D1144496

SHELLEY'S PLATONIC ANSWER TO A PLATONIC ATTACK ON POETRY

SHELLEY'S PLATONIC ANSWER TO A PLATONIC ATTACK ON POETRY

Joseph E. Baker, 1905-

UNIVERSITY OF IOWA PRESS ψ IOWA CITY

Contents

PREFACE

The evidence presented in this study, assembled in full force, seems sufficient to justify conclusions which, I must confess, surprised me when I first worked them out. Nothing would be served by listing here the interpretations of Shelley that now seem to me inadequate, some of which I myself once shared. For a brief survey of different estimates of Shelley's Platonism, one may turn, for example, to the fifth chapter of *The Deep Truth; a Study of Shelley's Scepticism,* by C. E. Pulos (Lincoln, Neb., 1954). Questions are raised there which this present treatise may help to answer. Pulos himself concludes (p. 88) "Shelley, then, is not a pseudo-Platonist but a Platonist in the sceptical tradition."

My investigations brought me by independent paths to a view similar to that of James A. Notopoulos's excellent volume, *The Platonism of Shelley, a Study of Platonism and the Poetic Mind,* (Durham, N.C., 1949), which includes a brief treatment of Shelley's prose but deals mainly with the poetry. This book by Notopoulos contains also a critical edition of Shelley's translations which I have compared with the passages I have used. My own references are, as far as possible, to common texts likely to be widely available. In my footnotes I have tied the knots that reticulate a wide net of indebtedness, point by point. Not the least of these are due to those many Platonists, of all varieties, who have contributed not only to learning but also to wisdom.

Iowa City, 1965   Joseph E. Baker

I. *Peacock and Plato*

It was not Irving Babbitt nor Bertrand Russell nor T. S. Eliot nor Cleanth Brooks nor any other twentieth-century critic of Romanticism who wrote the following:

Barbaric manners and supernatural interventions are [assumed by Romantics to be] essential to poetry. Either in the scene, or in the time, or in both, it must be remote from our ordinary perceptions. While the historian and the philosopher are advancing in, and accelerating, the progress of knowledge, the poet is wallowing in the rubbish of departed ignorance, and raking up the ashes of dead savages to find gewgaws and rattles for the grown babies of the age. Mr. Scott digs up the poachers and cattle-stealers of the ancient border. Lord Byron cruises for thieves and pirates on the shores of the Morea and among the Greek islands. Mr. Southey wades through ponderous volumes of travels and old chronicles, from which he carefully selects all that is false, useless, and absurd, as being essentially poetical; and when he has a commonplace book full of monstrosities, strings them into an epic. Mr. Wordsworth picks up village legends from old women and sextons; and Mr. Coleridge, to the valuable information acquired from similar sources, superadds the dreams of crazy theologians and the mysticisms of German metaphysics, and favors the world with visions in verse . . . .[1]

This is from "The Four Ages of Poetry" by Thomas Love Peacock, and it appeared in Ollier's *Literary Miscellany* in 1820. Plato had made a similar accusation in his day:

The imitative poet who aims at being popular is not by nature made, nor is his art intended, to please or to affect the rational principle in the soul; but he will prefer the passionate and fitful temper, which is easily imitated. . . . he awakens and nourishes and strengthens the feelings and impairs the reason . . . the imitator has no knowledge worth mentioning of what he imitates. Imitation is only a kind of play or sport . . . concerned with that which is thrice removed from the truth.[2]

---

[1] Peacock, "The Four Ages of Poetry," in Cook's edition of Shelley's *A Defense of Poetry* (Boston, 1891), p. 58.

[2] Plato, *Republic*, trans. Jowett, book X, sections 605A, 605B, 602B.

Peacock's strictures against romantic (and also against neo-classical) poetry are certainly of the earth earthy, though according to different tastes some might prefer to say that he is mud-slinging, and others that he has feet solidly on the ground. But Shelley in answering his friend quickly soars above that level, and soaring still doth sing the praises of poetry. He wrote to Peacock concerning "A Defence of Poetry" which he had ready to "dispatch by this post" and

which I design as an antidote to your "Four Ages of Poetry." You will see that I have taken a more general view of what is poetry than you have, and will perhaps agree with several of my positions, without considering your own touched. . . . I wish those who honour me with boxes [of books] would read and inwardly digest your "Four Ages of Poetry"; for I had much rather, for my own private reading, receive political, geological, and moral treatises than this stuff in *terza, ottava,* and *tremillesima rima* whose earthly baseness has attracted the lightning of undiscriminating censure upon the temple of immortal song.[3]

Though Shelley thus turns his gaze away from Peacock's censure, and does not seem to recognize that Plato attacked poetry at all, yet he is answering objections common to Plato and Peacock, and the structure of his "Defence" shows it—even after certain direct allusions to "The Four Ages of Poetry" were removed. Since Peacock's fling at poetry became important for its relation to Shelley, let us look at it through the poet's eyes, stating the features he would pick out to deal with. We can do this because the Bodleian MSS by Shelley include two drafts of portions of a letter to be sent to Ollier, the editor of the *Literary Miscellany*. Shelley wrote: "Mr. Editor—The following remarks were suggested by an essay entitled the Four Ages of Poetry which appeared some months since in your valuable Miscellany. . . . I suspect it to be written by a friend of mine who is a desperate rider of a hobby."[4] In spite of this last sentence, when he composed his "Defence" he knew perfectly well who wrote "The Four Ages of Poetry." But Shelley's idealistic admiration for Truth, with a capital T, did not keep him from lying to his public. On February 16, 1821, he sent to Ollier for publication his *Epipsychidion* whose "Advertisement," signed S, begins with this bald attempt to mislead: "The writer of the following lines died at Florence, as he was preparing for a voyage to one of the wildest

---

[3] Quoted in Cook's edition, *op. cit.*, p. 80.

[4] *Shelley's Prose in the Bodleian Manuscripts*, ed. A. H. Koszul (London, 1910), p. 120. Hereafter I shall refer to this book as Koszul, *op. cit.* Used by permission of the Clarendon Press, Oxford.

of the Sporades." Just the day before, on February 15, he wrote to Peacock that he had received a letter from him by boxes the Gisbornes sent by sea, and

I received at the same time your printed denunciations against general, and your written ones against particular, poetry . . . your anathemas against poetry itself excited me to a sacred rage, or *caloëthes scribendi* of vindicating the insulted Muses. I had the greatest possible desire to break a lance with you, within the lists of a magazine, in honour of my mistress Urania; but God willed that I should be too lazy. . . . Besides, I was at that moment reading Plato's *Ion*, which I recommend you to reconsider . . . . Among your anathemas of the modern attempts in poetry, do you include Keats's *Hyperion?* I think it very fine. His other poems are worth little . . . .[5]

This last statement may seem irrelevant to our present concern, but it is not. It comes as a shock to the reader who has taken *Adonais*, written a few weeks later, as a deeply sincere expression of profound admiration for Keats's poetry in general. This suggests that *Adonais* is not so much a lyrical outpouring of Shelley's own grief, as a public and Platonic defence of poets as such. As White says in his biography of Shelley, "In defending Keats, however, he was at the same time defending himself."[6] Keats died at Rome, February 23, while Shelley was preparing his answer to Peacock's "anathemas against poetry." The "Defence" and *Adonais* both may at times express not Shelley's lifelong convictions so much as certain appropriate Platonic principles, drawn, for example, from his reading, "at that moment," of the *Ion*, or from such Renaissance expressions of Platonism as Sidney's "Defense of Poesy." That Shelley had Sidney's work in mind can not be doubted by anyone who compares the many similar passages, as they are listed in parallel columns in Verkoren's dissertation.[7]

But it is not my primary purpose here to indicate each source of Shelley's ideas, even when such a source is Shelley's own previous writing—some of his debts being to himself, as Verkoren has shown. What Shelley's own long-range convictions may have been would raise biographical questions different from my present subject, which is rather to examine the position of the "Defence" itself, and the nature

---

[5] *Shelley's Literary and Philosophical Criticism*, ed. John Shawcross (London, 1909), pp. 212-214. Hereafter this volume will be referred to as Shawcross, *op. cit.* Used by permission of the Clarendon Press, Oxford.

[6] Newman I. White, *Shelley* (New York, 1940), II, 296.

[7] L. Verkoren, *A Study of Shelley's Defense of Poetry, its Origin* . . . (Amsterdam, 1937). He insists on Shelley's indebtedness to Sidney. The notes to Cook's edition list very many parallels.

of its critical philosophy. Where Shelley's earlier views illuminate his meaning, by contrast or similarity, they are relevant. But formulating the theory of his essay, and its tradition, is in itself a complicated problem. It is misleading to start with the assumption that the doctrine is going to be particularly Shelleyan. And it is even more misleading to take for granted that it will voice "Romantic Platonism." In the first place, Shelley's ideas are often the opposite of those typical of "Romanticism" as defined by students of Continental literature shortly before and shortly after 1800. In a sense it is true that just as there are several varieties of Christianity, so there are several varieties of Platonism—Epicurean, Puritanical, Rationalistic, Catholic, Liberal, Romantic, etc. But it is necessary to show where Shelley's "Defence of Poetry" stands in relation to these different manifestations of Platonism, not merely to one which is peculiar to the poet's own epoch, or to his own temperament.

Plato had said in the *Republic* (568 B, Taylor's translation) that tragic poets should not be admitted into the ideal state because they are "panegyrists of Tyranny." Peacock says that in origin, in the Iron Age, the productions of poets were

panegyrical . . . of a few pre-eminent individuals. They tell us how many battles such an one has fought, how many helmets he has cleft . . . how many widows he has made, how much land he has appropriated, how many houses he has demolished for other people, what a large one he has built for himself . . . and how liberally and plentifully he pays, feeds, and intoxicates the divine and immortal bards . . . .[8]

Shelley's method of reply is illustrated in his bland observation that "to such purposes [as flattery] poetry cannot be made subservient"; and where Plato had accused Euripides, he cites rather Addison's *Cato*, and explains

But in periods of the decay of social life, the drama sympathizes with that decay. Tragedy becomes a cold imitation of the form of the great masterpieces of antiquity . . . or a weak attempt to teach certain doctrines, which the writer considers as moral truths; and which are usually no more than specious flatteries of some gross vice or weakness . . . .[9]

And in his "Defence" he has set out to counteract Peacock by offering

---

[8] *Four Ages*, p. 48.

[9] Page references for the "Defence of Poetry" are to *Shelley: Selected Poems, Essays, and Letters*, ed. Ellsworth Barnard (New York, 1944), where some of Shelley's critical prose is conveniently included in the same volume with his best poems. (Used by permission of the Odyssey Press.) The present reference is to p. 545.

[4]

a rival interpretation of the history of poetry in different ages. "In the infancy of the world, neither poets themselves nor their auditors are fully aware of the excellence of poetry."[10] Still earlier in the "Defence" he has discussed "the nature itself of language, which is a more direct representation of the actions and passions of our internal being . . . than colour, form, or motion."[11] Thus the first part of the "Defence" is a reply to the first of the "positions" of Peacock as Shelley read "The Four Ages of Poetry." In the fragment found with the Bodleian MS sources of "A Defence of Poetry" we read Shelley's own summary of Peacock's "opinion." At first poetry

was no more than the rude efforts of expression . . . before language had assumed any degree of philosophical perfection; and instead of softening the manners and refining the feelings of the semi-barbarians whose intervals of repose it soothed, it flattered their vices and hardened them to fresh acts of carnage and destruction.[12]

It is not clear in the MS what Shelley intended to designate next, as the second point made by Peacock. Perhaps because the second of the Four Ages was "the age of Homer, the golden age of poetry," which even Peacock admired, Shelley had not completely formulated his second point of disagreement with his friend. But just before his *thirdly* in his fragmentary outline he does mention the hostile view that "The character and personal conduct of the poets themselves . . . was then deserving of contempt." This explains why he breaks into his historical survey to argue against the "whole objection . . . of the immorality of poetry" which

rests upon a misconception of the manner in which poetry acts to produce the moral improvement of man. Ethical science arranges the elements which poetry has created . . . . But poetry acts in another and a diviner manner. It awakens and enlarges the mind itself by rendering it the receptacle of a thousand unapprehended combinations of thought.[13]

---

[10] "Defence," p. 538.

[11] *Ibid.*, p. 534.

[12] Koszul, *op. cit.*, p. 118.

[13] "Defence," p. 539. Attempts to grasp the general *Gestalt* of a piece of literature can go wrong through lack of biographical evidence concerning the author's plan. For example, Cook's "Analysis" or outline at the end of his edition of Shelley's "Defence" makes "historical review of European poetry" merely a subdivision under "The Effects of Poetry," omits from this "Historical review" everything before "The perfection of the lyric and the drama at Athens," and begins the division "The Diviner Sources and Effects of Poetry" two pages after Shelley's actual shift from Peacock to the *Ion* with the sentence "Poetry is indeed something divine." To other readers Shelley's essay has seemed planless.

This is inserted, as it were, into the midst of his treatment of Homer, though he reserves his most enthusiastic praise of the morality and divinity of poets and poetry until after he has disposed of the four points he found in Peacock's "treatise," and is ready to turn to the *Ion* for positive doctrine. That this was Shelley's general plan is evident, for Mr. A. H. Koszul found with the Bodleian manuscript sources of "A Defence of Poetry" not only this sketchy summary of Peacock's "Four Ages," but also fragments from a translation of Plato's *Ion* which differs from Shelley's published translation of the *Ion* in ways whose significance we will note later. Analyzing Peacock's essay and "the paradox it attempts to support," Shelley continues to formulate what he disagrees with:

3rdly With the progress of civil society and the developement of the arts of life poetry has deteriorated in exact proportion to the universal amelioration; and the examples (afforded by it) in ages of high (refinement and civilization) and especially in the age in which we live, are below derision and the instruments of the utmost passiveness and depravity of moral sentiment.[14]

Amusing illustrations of this may be found in Peacock's indictment. In the third, the silver age, poetry, fastidious and elegant, finally has nothing to offer but "commonplace, which at length becomes thoroughly wearisome."

But there is always a multitude of listless idlers, yawning for amusement, and gaping for novelty; and the poet makes it his glory to be foremost among their purveyors. Then comes the age of brass, which, by rejecting the polish and the learning of the age of silver, and taking a retrograde stride to the barbarisms and crude traditions of the age of iron, professes to return to nature and revive the age of gold. This is the second childhood of poetry. To the comprehensive energy of the Homeric Muse, which, by giving at once the grand outline of things, presented to the mind a vivid picture in one or two verses, inimitable alike in simplicity and magnificence, is substituted a verbose and minutely-detailed description of thoughts, passions, actions, persons, and things, in that loose, rambling style of verse . . . [though the best poetry of this type] contains many passages of exceeding beauty in the midst of masses of amplification and repetition.[15]

Such poetry "flourished in the decline of the Roman Empire"—and this chaos has come again, for "Modern poetry has also its four ages," beginning with the age of chivalry when "the character of every true

---

[14] Koszul, *op. cit.*, p. 119. The phrases I have placed in parentheses were cancelled.

[15] *Four Ages*, pp. 53-54.

man" was compounded of "the three staple ingredients of lover, prize-fighter, and fanatic." In our golden age, carried "farthest of all by Shakespeare and his contemporaries," he finds "the old English drama very picturesque . . . though it is a picture of nothing that was ever seen on earth." Therefore, the "greatest of English poets" is Milton, standing "alone between the ages of gold and silver, combining the excellences of both." The "reign of authority" during the silver age was finally shaken by "the subtle scepticism of Hume, the solemn irony of Gibbon, the daring paradoxes of Rousseau, and the biting ridicule of Voltaire."[16] Shelley in his "Defence" mentioned these four men—plus Locke—and in his manuscript added "I follow the classification adopted by the author of the Four Ages of Poetry." But he is unhappy about the inclusion of Rousseau, "essentially a poet" among these "mere reasoners." Shelley then shows how far he has come from the eighteenth-century radicalism of his *Queen Mab* by deprecating the importance of these men, whom Peacock had called "deep and elaborate thinkers." Shelley replies:

Yet it is easy to calculate the degree of moral and intellectual improvement which the world would have exhibited, had they never lived. . . . But it exceeds all imagination to conceive what would have been the moral condition of the world if neither Dante, Petrarch, Boccaccio, Chaucer, Shakespeare, Calderon, Lord Bacon, nor Milton, had ever existed; if Raphael and Michael Angelo had never been born; if the Hebrew poetry had never been translated; if a revival of the study of Greek literature had never taken place.[17]

To these Renaissance expressions of the "creative faculty itself" he ascribes even the fact that the human mind was "awakened to the invention of the grosser sciences, and that application of analytic reasoning to the aberrations of society, which it is now attempted to exalt" above the poetic faculty. It may be noted that not one French name appears in Shelley's listing of the great. But Shelley's disagreement with Peacock was sharpest where his friend "would undervalue contemporary merit." His "Defence," as we have it, was conceived of as merely the first part of a work, the second part of which would "have for its object an application of these principles to the present state of the cultivation of poetry."[18] Peacock's essay had said that now the poetic "patriarchs of the age of brass,"

16 *Ibid.*, pp. 54-56.
17 "Defence," p. 559.
18 *Ibid.*, pp. 567-568.

[7]

mistaking the prominent novelty for the all-important totality, seem to have ratiocinated much in the following manner: "Poetical genius is the finest of all things, and we feel that we have more of it than anyone ever had. The way to bring it to perfection is to cultivate poetical impressions exclusively. Poetical impressions can be received only among natural scenes, for all that is artificial is anti-poetical. Society is artificial, therefore we will live out of society. The mountains are natural, therefore we will live in the mountains. There we shall be shining models of purity and virtue, passing the whole day in the innocent and amiable occupation of going up and down hill, receiving poetical impressions, and communicating them in immortal verse to admiring generations." To some such perversion of intellect we owe that egregious confraternity of rimesters, known by the name of the Lake Poets . . . [who] remaining studiously ignorant of history, society, and human nature, cultivated the fantasy only at the expense of the memory and the reason.[19]

Could Peacock have had in mind especially Shelley's Preface to "The Revolt of Islam" (1817)? It contains the following passage, more "egregious" than any critical utterance by Wordsworth or Coleridge:

There is an education preculiarly fitted for a Poet . . . . The circumstances of my accidental education have been favourable to this ambition. I have been familiar from boyhood with mountains and lakes and the sea, and the solitude of forests . . . . I have sailed down mighty rivers, and seen the sun rise and set, and the stars come forth, whilst I have sailed night and day down a rapid stream among mountains.[20]

How silly this is, compared with his "Defence of Poetry," written a mere four years later, but after Shelley had soaked himself in Plato!

Some of Peacock's judgments are Classical, and have been variously expressed, with more dignity and less liveliness, by such critics as Paul Elmer More, T. S. Eliot, Dr. Johnson, even Coleridge. Concerning some of the romantic fantasies touched by Peacock, Classicists might say in the words of Shelley's *Hellas*, "killing Truth had glared on them."[21] This raises the problem of the relation of truth and poetry, which R. P. Warren calls "the very central and crucial critical issue of the period."[22] From the seventeenth century to the twentieth this problem has been recognized to involve the nature of language. Peacock declares:

Feeling and passion are best painted in, and roused by, ornamental and figurative language; but the reason and the understanding are best ad-

---

19 *Four Ages*, pp. 56-57.
20 Shelley, *Selected Poems* . . . , ed. Barnard, p. 523.
21 Line 234.
22 Coleridge, *The Rime of the Ancient Mariner*, with an essay by Robert Penn Warren (New York, 1946), p. 101.

dressed in the simplest and most unvarnished phrase. Pure reason and dispassionate truth would be perfectly ridiculous in verse, as we may judge by versifying one of Euclid's demonstrations. . . . Thus the empire of thought is withdrawn from poetry, as the empire of facts had been before.[23]

Peacock was merely restating what had been said many times before. Basil Willey quotes many passages of similar tenor in *The Seventeenth Century Background, Studies in the Thought of the Age in Relation to Poetry and Religion,* e.g., from Thomas Sprat's *History of the Royal Society,* published a hundred and fifty-three years before Peacock's essay. And Willey adds, "It was not only from the Cartesian universe, but also from Plato's Republic, that poetry was banished."[24] The last sentence of Shelley's manuscript notes for a letter to Ollier on *The Four Ages of Poetry* reads, "Before we subject these propositions to (analysis) it were well to discover what poetry is." Hence in his "Defence" he treats this subject first, and then moves to his rival sketch of the development of poetry, with the transition sentence, "Having determined what is poetry, and who are poets, let us proceed to estimate its effects upon society." For that is the real purpose of the survey of poetical history. And proceeding with his reply in due order he arrives at Peacock's point which Shelley in his manuscript letter to Ollier had designated as

4thly Every person conscious of intellectual power ought studiously to wean himself from the study and practice of poetry, and ought to apply that power to general finance, political economy, to the study in short [of] the laws according to which the forms of the social order might be most wisely regulated for the happiness of those whom it binds together. (These are indeed high objects, and I pledge myself to worship Themis rather than Apollo . . . .)[25]

This last sentence has been cancelled, but it is not insignificant, as we shall see when we have noted the social considerations that Shelley deems necessary to justify the ways of poetry to man. And it accords with what he had already written to Peacock, January 26, 1819, that he considered poetry "very subordinate to moral and political science."[26]

---

[23] *Four Ages,* pp. 52-53.

[24] Willey, *Seventeenth Century Background* (London, 1934), p. 88. In the forefront of Sprat's account is the intention to get rid of many "errors of antiquity—'And to accomplish this, they have endeavour'd, to separate the knowledge of Nature from the colours of Rhetorick, the devices of Fancy, or the delightful deceit of Fables.'—in a word, they have determined to declare war upon poetry." (pp. 210-211)

[25] Koszul, *op. cit.,* p. 119. "Defence," p. 537.

[26] *Letters of Percy Bysshe Shelley,* ed. Ingpen (London, 1909), II, 660.

He has not misrepresented *The Four Ages*, which had come to the following conclusions as to poetry:

It can never make a philosopher, nor a statesman, nor in any class of life a useful or rational man. It cannot claim the slightest share in any one of the comforts and utilities of life, of which we have witnessed so many and so rapid advances. . . . There are more good poems already existing than are sufficient to employ that portion of life which any mere reader and recipient of poetical impressions should devote to them. . . . To read the promiscuous rubbish of the present time, to the exclusion of the select treasures of the past, is to substitute the worse for the better variety of the same mode of enjoyment.

But in whatever degree poetry is cultivated, it must necessarily be to the neglect of some branch of useful study; and it is a lamentable spectacle to see minds capable of better things running to seed in the specious indolence of these empty, aimless mockeries of intellectual exertion. . . . We may easily conceive that the day is not distant when the degraded state of every species of poetry will be as generally recognized as that of dramatic poetry has long been . . . because intellectual power and intellectual acquisition have turned themselves into other and better channels . . . .[27]

Thus Peacock wavers between a rationalist's discrimination and a utilitarian's hostile exclusion of poetry from subjects of serious concern. His essay would sound very "modern" today to those who wish to exclude from learning and statesmanship everything that cannot be called "scientific," and it would have sounded very sensible three centuries ago to extreme advocates of the new science. It has been the function of English defenders of poetry from Sir Philip Sidney to Matthew Arnold to urge the Anglo-Saxon mind beyond its utilitarian preoccupations and its tendency toward more or less disguised Puritanism. Of all the classic defences, Shelley's is the most Platonic, though it answers an attack that was close to Plato in the ways already indicated, and as the following passages illustrate:

The philosophic mental tranquillity which looks round with an equal eye on all external things, collects a store of ideas, discriminates their relative value, assigns to all their proper place, and from the materials of useful knowledge thus collected, appreciated, and arranged, forms new combinations that impress the stamp of their power and utility on the real business of life, is diametrically the reverse of that frame of mind which poetry inspires, or from which poetry can emanate . . . it is not to the thinking and studious, and scientific and philosophical part of the community, not to those whose minds are bent on the pursuit and promotion of permanently useful ends and aims, that poets must address their minstrelsy, but to that

---

[27] *Four Ages*, pp. 59-61.

much larger portion of the reading public whose minds are not awakened to the desire of valuable knowledge, and who are indifferent to anything beyond being charmed, moved, . . . excited by passion . . . which is the commotion of a weak and selfish mind; pathos, which is the whining of an unmanly spirit; and sublimity, which is the inflation of an empty head . . . .

We shall be right in refusing to admit [the poet] into a well-ordered State, because he awakens and nourishes and strengthens the feelings and impairs the reason. As in a city when the evil are permitted to have authority and the good are put out of the way, so in the soul of man, we maintain, the imitative poet implants an evil constitution, for he indulges the irrational nature which has no discernment of greater and less, but thinks the same thing at one time great and at another small—he is a manufacturer of images and is very far removed from the truth. . . . The best of us, as I conceive, when we listen to a passage of Homer, or one of the tragedians, in which he represents some pitiful hero who is drawling out his sorrows in a long oration, or weeping, and smiting his breast—the best of us, you know, delight in giving way to sympathy. . . . Lust and anger and all the other affections, of desire and pain and pleasure, which are held to be inseparable from every action—in all of them poetry feeds and waters the passions instead of drying them up.

The first of these passages is from Peacock's essay, the second from Plato's *Republic*,[28] while his *Ion*, which Shelley was reading at that time, comes near to implying that sublimity is "the inflation of an empty head." The genius of Plato, like that of England, is on one side rationalistic, Puritanical, and utilitarian; on the other side artistic, gay, imaginative.

Shelley had, as I have said, soaked himself in Plato. He had just recently written to Peacock, in November of 1820, "I have been reading nothing but Greek and Spanish. Plato and Calderon have been my gods."[29] His friend, Hogg, tells us, "In his short life, and without ostentation, he had in truth read more Greek than many an aged pedant. . . . A pocket edition of Plato, of Plutarch, of Euripides, without interpretation or notes . . . was his ordinary companion, and he read the text straightforward for hours."[30] At Oxford, says Hogg, he read Sydenham's translation of the *Republic* "with infinite pleasure,"[31] and in 1812 he de-

---

28 *Ibid.*, and *Republic*, trans. Jowett, X, 605, 606. Cf: "For Plato, reality is rational, scientific and logical, or it is nothing. The poetic medium forms a kind of refracting screen which disguises and distorts reality and . . . [appeals] to the shallowest of our sensibilities." Eric Havelock, *Preface to Plato* (Cambridge, Mass. 1963) pp. 25-26.
29 Shawcross, *op. cit.*, p. 211.
30 T. J. Hogg, *Life of Percy Bysshe Shelley* (London, 1858), I, 127.
31 *Ibid.*, 192.

clared a preference "that the Greek classics should have Latin or English versions printed opposite."[32] At that time, "We had," says Hogg, "several of the publications of the learned and eccentric Platonist, Thomas Taylor" (whose translations of Plato appeared along with those of Sydenham). At first,

our knowledge of Plato was derived solely from Dacier's translation of a few of the dialogues, and from an English version of the French translation: We had never attempted a single sentence in Greek. Since that time, however, I believe, few of our countrymen have read the golden works of that majestic philosopher in the original language more frequently and more carefully than ourselves.[33]

But it was "not strictly true" that "Shelley had not read any portion of Plato in the original before he went to Italy"; he had a very legible edition of Plato's works, "Bipont, I think. I remember going to London with him, and we read a good deal of it together. Phaedrus, I am pretty sure."[34] Thus, before he went to Italy he had known Plato in Greek, in Ficino's Latin, Dacier's French, Taylor and Sydenham's English, not to mention the renascent Plato of Spenser, Milton, Bacon, Sidney. To these interpretations and translations he added his own translations. In October, 1821, he writes Hogg that he has translated the *Symposium*, *Ion*, and the first part of the *Phaedo*.[35] These dialogues, and the *Phaedrus* which he began to study years before, are the ones which set forth most clearly the central ideas of his "Defence," written early in 1821. We may add the *Republic*, from which we have some fragments of translation by Shelley. And with the manuscript of the "Defence" Koszul found that Shelley had "transcribed the delightful passage in Plato's *Leges* (ii. 653-654) which contrasts the disordinate cries and motions of children and animals with the human aspirations after rhythm and harmony, and attributes the latter to the teaching of the Muses, Apollo, and Dionysos."[36] Shelley makes use of this passage in the second paragraph of his "Defence." Thus his own essay moves from a passage in

---

[32] *Letters*, ed. Ingpen, I, 373-374.
[33] Hogg, *op. cit.*, I, 191-192, 103.
[34] *Ibid.*, 192-193. J. A. Notopoulos, in *Modern Language Review*, XXXIV (1939), 421, states that "The text which Shelley used" in translating the *Symposium* was "the Bipont edition of Plato"—*cum Marsilii Ficini Interpretatione*. And (p. 422), "The juxtaposition of Ficino's Latin translation to the Greek text aided Shelley considerably . . . and partly accounts for the speed" of the translating, started "on 9 July and finished . . . 17 July, 1818."
[35] Shelley, *Complete Works*, ed. Ingpen and Peck (London, 1926-30), VII, 311.
[36] Koszul, *op. cit.*, p. 122.

the *Laws* to a passage in the *Ion;* and pertinent translations from both were found with the manuscript.

Almost all the important dialogues of Plato had been translated into English by Thomas Taylor—but *not* the *Ion* or the *Symposium.* Possibly Shelley, in choosing to translate these, wished to supplement the Platonic works available in good English. This may be taken as evidence that he had read and admired Taylor's Plato. But I have not been able to prove this by parallels between his phrases and those of Taylor, for example in Taylor's *Phaedrus.* Even when the thought is identical, Shelley gives it his own phrasing. Indeed, there is no better illustration of Shelley's originality of expression than to notice that when he borrows an idea, he puts it into his own words.

Shelley's admiration for Plato could hardly be surpassed. He pays him the supreme compliment, in the Prologue to his *Hellas,* by having Christ himself speak of

> Plato's sacred light,
> Of which my spirit was a burning morrow—

By the time Shelley wrote his "Defence of Poetry" he was familiar with Plato's treatments of literature, and was a profound admirer of Plato's philosophy. To what extent do their literary theories agree?

II. *Poetry to be Judged by Moral and "Spiritual" Criteria*

In one version of his proposed letter to Ollier, Shelley had expressed admiration for Peacock's "high objects," (though not his theories) and had pledged himself to worship not Apollo but Themis, the goddess of law, justice, and universal order. Anyone who had read the biographies of Shelley and not his "Defence of Poetry" might think this a whimsical paradox. Actually, it is very appropriate. Keats had praised the bards who hold the British Isles in fealty to Apollo, god of Beauty; and the earliest English aesthetes took their start from Keats. But Shelley's cult was to be among the seekers of social justice. Shelley never implies that in the criticism of poetry only aesthetic effects are to be considered. He, like most of the Romantics, agrees with Marxist and with Humanist critics, that literature is ultimately to be judged according to moral, "spiritual," and political criteria. He never uses the art-for-art's-sake defence of poetry, that social effects are irrelevant to a criticism of art as such. He took his stand on the same ground as Plato—and Peacock, to whom he had written two years earlier (in the midst of composing *Prometheus Unbound*)—that he considered poetry very subordinate to moral and political science.

In *The Witch of Atlas* (completed in August, 1820, halfway between *Prometheus* and the "Defence") he writes that some things are

> Not to be mirrored in a holy song—
> Distortions foul of supernatural awe,
> And pale imaginings of visioned wrong;   (538-540)

This agrees precisely with Plato. Among the few passages the poet translated from the *Republic* are the following:

And first, we must improve upon the composers of fabulous histories in verse, to compose them according to the rules of moral beauty; and those not composed according to the rules must be rejected; and we must persuade mothers and nurses to teach those which we approve to their children, and to form their minds by moral fables, far more than their bodies by their hands.

Plato cites "imaginings of visioned wrong" supposed to be committed by the gods as "distortions foul." Then Plato says, as Shelley translates:

God then, since he is good, cannot be, as is vulgarly supposed, the cause of all things; he is the cause, indeed, of very few things. Among the great variety of events which happen in the course of human affairs, evil prodigiously overbalances good in everything which regards men. Of all that is good there can be no other cause than God; but some other cause ought to be discovered for evil, which should never be imputed as an effect to God.

Nor must we restrict the poets alone to an exhibition of the example of virtuous manners . . . but all other artists.

In a note, Shelley compares the art of the early and the late Classical period to the manners of their respective times, adding, "With a liberal interpretation, a similar analogy might be extended into literary composition,"[37] and this he does in his "Defence." In the preface to *Prometheus Unbound* he stated as his purpose, "to familiarise the highly refined imagination of the more select classes of poetical readers with beautiful idealisms of moral excellence; aware,"—he continues—that "reasoned principles of moral conduct" will be seeds sown by the wayside and trodden down, until the mind has the Christian virtue to trust, hope, and love, and he adds "admire" and "endure." *Prometheus Unbound* itself holds up to admiration a Christ-like figure that endures, and who utters in the first act the Platonic warning, (450) "Methinks I grow like what I contemplate." This is a rephrasing of Shelley's much earlier line, "The mind becomes that which it contemplates," in Part II (15) of *Prince Athanase* (1817), called at first *Pandemos and Urania* from Pausanias' speech in Plato's *Symposium*. In the "Defence" he speaks of us "becoming a portion of that beauty which we contemplate."[38] This is the Platonic social psychology back of the desire to *restrict* the artist to fair sights and sounds.[39] Often we do find such restrictions limiting the productions of the Romantics, but not of Homer, Aeschylus,

---

[37] Shelley, *Essays, Letters from Abroad, Translations and Fragments,* ed. Mrs. Shelley (London, 1840), I, 308-309, 312, 313. (*Republic,* II, 377, 379; III, 401.) Notopoulos's "Critical Edition" in the first passage above has "we must impose" instead of "we must improve." (Part III of *The Platonism of Shelley* [Durham, N.C., 1949], p. 496.)

[38] "Defence," p. 552.

[39] The *locus classicus* for this view is the *Republic,* book III.

Aristophanes, Dante, Shakespeare, Michelangelo, Rembrandt.[40] Few authors have gone farther than Shelley in the actual practice of excluding the ugly and portraying the beautiful. He has been criticized, for example, as to *Prometheus Unbound* itself, for not showing any struggle, any real resistance on the part of the evil tryant. But that is not an artistic failure in carrying out his intent; it is an artistic success in avoiding what he did not believe in, the dissemination of "images of moral deformity."[41] He believed in showing the idealistic virtues of endurance and forgiveness—"moral excellence"—and the shimmering utopia that is to be. Both the priggishness and the sentimentalism of Shelley spring from a reluctance to use poetic art to portray the ugly, or the ridiculous. He has the support of Plato's theory. Not only tragedy and Homeric epic, but comedy also was to be excluded from the Republic, "Neither ought our guardians to be given to laughter."[42] Shelley said to Hogg, "I am convinced that there can be no entire regeneration of mankind until laughter is put down."[43] It is not usually observed that Shelley's faults are sometimes Platonic, as well as many of his virtues. Plato's own realism in practice, his skill in writing high intellectual comedy and in portraying the ridiculous (as in the character of Euthyphro), seem to have escaped Shelley's notice. The poet's own practice, his humorlessness and pervasive tenuousness, in contrast to the solider creative art of Plato, constitute a rather effective demonstration of the error in Plato's over-idealistic theory. Plato would have admitted Shelley to his Republic while excluding Shakespeare, for he says

When any one of these pantomimic gentlemen, who are so clever that they can imitate anything, comes to us, and makes a proposal to exhibit himself and his poetry, we will fall down and worship him as a sweet and holy and wonderful being; but we must also inform him that in our State such as he are not permitted to exist . . . .

And we are ready to acknowledge that Homer is the greatest of poets and first of tragedy writers; but we must remain firm in our conviction that hymns to the gods and praises of famous men are the only poetry which ought to be admitted into our State.[44]

Hymns to such entities as the West Wind or poetic dramas and narratives which successfully "imitate the style of the virtuous only" would

---

[40] See Cleanth Brooks, *Modern Poetry and the Tradition, (passim.)*
[41] *Republic*, trans. Jowett, III, 401C.
[42] *Ibid.*, 388E.
[43] White, *Shelley*, I, 309.
[44] *Republic*, trans. Jowett, III, 398; X, 607A.

[16]

surely qualify Shelley for admittance where Plato's standards are most exclusive.

In the Preface to *Prometheus Unbound* Shelley mentions his purpose to write "a systematical history of what appear to me to be the genuine elements of human society," in which, he warns, "let not the advocates of injustice and superstition flatter themselves that I should take Aeschylus rather than Plato as my model." (He evidently recognizes the difference between the attitude toward the rebel exhibited in his own *Prometheus* and that of Aeschylus.) In his "Defence of Poetry" he has devoted a large part of the essay to setting forth a philosophy of history that in many respects is a striking anticipation of that of Carlyle—except that Carlyle is closer to the spirit of Aeschylus.

When he is using social and moral criteria to judge literary values, Shelley is in agreement with Peacock and with Plato—and, we may add, with most of the critics during the Renaissance, Puritan, Neo-Classical, Romantic, and Victorian periods, and in the twentieth century with critical schools as different as the Neo-Humanist, the Marxist, and the Nationalist. Longinus's view, that "the Sublime is an image reflected from the inward greatness of the soul,"[45] is echoed, perhaps unconsciously, in Shelley's "the greatest poets have been men of the most spotless virtue, of the most consummate prudence . . ."[46] And there is a hint of such an attitude in the *Republic* and in the second book of Plato's *Laws*. [47]

---

[45] Trans. William Smith, 5th ed. (London, 1800), IX; or, as in the Loeb translation, the "true ring of a noble mind."

[46] "Defence," p. 565.

[47] *Laws*, II, 655-659. Cf. *Republic*, III, 400E.

III. *Further: Poetry, as such, Defined by Moral Criteria*

Starting with the principle that the judging of literature must be more social than aesthetic, how then can Plato ban the poets from his ideal Republic while Shelley sings their praises? E.g. "The great instrument of moral good is the [poetic] imagination,"[48] and the poet "is the author to others of the highest wisdom" and "virtue."[49] Contrast Plato's protest against the claim that Homer "is profitable for education and the ordering of human things, and that you should take him up again and again and get to know him and regulate your whole life according to him."[50]

By Shelley, moral criteria are used not only to evaluate, but to *define* poetry. In one sense, he is the more austere, in theory. A poet of the wrong kind would be banned by Plato; he would not even be called a poet by Shelley. For that the poet "is the wisest, the happiest, and the best" of men, "inasmuch as he is a poet, is," according to Shelley, "incontrovertible."[51] He still insists on the moral value of the poetic power when, in the last paragraph of the "Defence," he grants that as to individual poets his praise may be controvertible, that "The persons in whom this power resides may often, as far as regards many portions of their nature, have little apparent correspondence with that spirit of good of which they are the ministers. But even whilst they deny and abjure, they are yet compelled to serve, the power which is seated on the throne of their own soul." At this point, Shelley, in danger of agreeing with the *Republic* concerning the moral worth of poets, has found in the doctrine of the *Ion* a starting-hole to hide him from this open and apparent shame!

---

48 "Defence," p. 540.
49 *Ibid.*, p. 565.
50 *Republic*, trans. Jowett, X, 606E, 607.
51 "Defence," p. 565.

[18]

Could Shelley have considered himself a prudent, happy man? In his poetry he falls "upon the thorns of life," he bleeds. In *Adonais*, written immediately after the "Defence," he portrays himself as "one frail form, A phantom among men; companionless," exiled, "neglected, and apart," with branded brow "like Cain's" or, he adds, like Christ's. He has indeed performed the function of the poet which he had just outlined in prose, but as a result of this imprudence

> now he fled astray
> With feeble steps o'er the world's wilderness
> And his own thoughts, along that rugged way,
> Pursued, like raging hounds, their father and their prey.[52]

His disagreement elsewhere with his own "Defence" is not confined to remarks about himself. Of Wordsworth he had said, "That such a man should be such a poet!" He wrote to John and Maria Gisborne, July 19, 1821, "The poet and the man are two different natures; though they exist together they may be unconscious of each other . . ."[53]

But his "Defence" is not an autobiographical lyric. In this great prose work he is expressing the view common to the Platonists who, unlike Plato himself, have glorified "the poet." Thus Sidney considers poetry to be higher than any of the "serving sciences" and poets to have "a most just title to be princes over all the rest," certainly above historians, philosophers, or lawyers.[54] Shelley places the fame of poets on a level not surpassed by that of legislators or even founders of religion, though these others may win celebrity with "their flattery of the gross opinions of the vulgar."[55] Thus he carries on a tradition which of course contradicts Plato who, in his *Phaedrus*, assigns "the character of a poet" to the sixth place down, two ranks below the gymnast and only two above the sophist and demagogue; while among those souls who have "seen most of truth" he places near the top the "righteous king or warrior chief" and the "politician, or economist, or trader."[56] Peacock and the utilitarians in general agree much more closely with Plato, literally, than any of the Platonists from Plotinus to Emerson and Arnold; hardly any follower of Plato has followed him in this respect.

---

[52] Stanzas, XXXI-XXXIV.

[53] *Letters*, ed. Ingpen, II, 883.

[54] Sidney, "The Defense of Poesy otherwise known as An Apology for Poetry," ed. A. S. Cook (Boston, 1890), pp. 12-15. This will be referred to hereafter as *Apology*.

[55] "Defence," p. 534.

[56] *Phaedrus*, trans. Jowett, 248.

Platonists may claim that in treating poetry Plato made a mistake, and that to his error there is a Platonic answer, more in accord with his own principles, certainly more in accord with his own spirit. "Plato was essentially a poet," says Shelley,[57] agreeing in this with ancient admirers of Plato. Proclus remarked that Plato was as good a poet as Homer and would have been expelled from his own Republic. And "Longinus finds a forerunner in Plato. . . . For the strength of Platonism lies in the fact that it is not a creed but an inspiration, flowing in diverse channels."[58] The twentieth-century American Platonist and critic, Paul Elmer More, asserts concerning Proclus's great predecessor,

Plotinus made a valuable correction to the doctrine of Ideas, and may be said, without quibbling, to have been more Platonic than Plato. . . . Why . . . did not Plato, taught by his own technique, understand that the great artist has his eye fastened not on nature or manufactured objects as on an opaque veil, but is really looking through these to the Ideas behind the curtain?

This question was answered by Plotinus in such a way that "he justified Platonism as the artist's philosophy *par excellence*."[59] Yet we must notice that Plotinus, Proclus, Ficino, Sidney, Shelley, Emerson, Arnold, Paul Elmer More, all succeeded in correcting Plato without losing their reverence for Plato's philosophy; indeed their own critical principles could not have been constructed except on the foundation laid by their master.

---

[57] "Defence," p. 535.
[58] E. E. Sikes, *The Greek View of Poetry* (London, 1931), pp. 238, 211.
[59] P. E. More, *Hellenistic Philosophies* (Princeton, 1923), pp. 184-185.

IV. *Identification of the True, the Good, the Beautiful*

The assumption that poetry is better *as poetry* if it has social virtue, is based on Plato's ultimate identification of "the true and the beautiful, in a word, the good"—to make use of Shelley's phrasing.[60] Shelley carried on this process of identification by adding liberal democracy, which he also considered Platonic. As early as *Alastor* (dated 1815) "a veiled maid . . . Herself a poet," and withal something of an Idea of intellectual beauty veiled for mortal sight, sang, with the "voice of his own soul," and we find the Platonic trinity,

> Knowledge and truth and virtue were her theme,
> And lofty hopes of divine liberty,
> Thoughts the most dear to him, and poesy[61]

Later he combines his interest in science, his worship of the god of poetry, and a metaphor, "the light of truth," which has persisted throughout the history of Platonic thought, into his *Hymn of Apollo* (written 1820). And since Beauty is Truth, the god of the arts can say —Poetry can say (italics mine):

> The sunbeams are *my* shafts, with which I kill
> Deceit, that loves the night and fears the day;
>   . . . . . .
>   and from the glory of my ray
> *Good minds and open actions* take new might,
>   . . . . . .
> All harmony of instrument or verse,
>   *All prophecy*, all medicine is mine,
>   *All light* of art or nature;

Book VI of the *Republic* and the Myth of the Cave in the following

---

[60] "Defence," p. 532.
[61] *Alastor*, lines 151-161. As to Shelley's ascription of democracy to Plato, see below.

[21]

book supply the classic elaboration of this metaphor of enlightenment. It has been more than a figure of speech; for it has helped to cast a glamour around duty and around the hard technical work of art; and it has encouraged lovers of beauty to interest themselves in the pursuit of truth. This is one of those concepts popularized by Christianity, which, according to Shelley, "in its abstract purity, became the exoteric expression of the esoteric doctrines of the poetry and wisdom of antiquity," i.e. of Plato, to whose "moral and intellectual system of doctrine" he is here referring.[62] More recent Platonists have agreed with Shelley in tracing such connections. Dean W. R. Inge says, "Our creeds are the formulae of victorious Platonism,"[63] and "it will probably be forever impossible to cut Platonism out of Christianity."[64] Muirhead says, "Platonism might indeed be called the intellectual side of Christianity."[65] The Platonic opening of the Gospel of John—so frequently followed by nineteenth- and twentieth-century traditionalists like Coleridge, Arnold, Inge, P. E. More—asserts that the *Logos* (meaning both Reason and Word) "was the true Light, which lighteth every man that cometh into the world," and in this "life was the light of men." In much the same way Shelley calls poetry "the light of life; the source of whatever of beautiful or generous or true can have place in an evil time."[66] "That Light whose smile kindles the Universe" is "That Beauty in which all things work and move," identified with a "sustaining Love" woven "through the web of being." These phrases are from stanza LIV of *Adonais*, which is followed by mention of "The breath whose might I have invoked in song," equivalent of the "holy light" invoked by Milton at the beginning of Book III of *Paradise Lost*, "since God is light . . . Bright effluence of bright essence," or a "stream Whose Fountain who shall tell?" doubtless the "burning fountain" of *Adonais* (line 338).

Without maintaining that Shelley in his intellectual career passes by definite stages from consistent naturalism to consistent Platonism,

---

[62] "Defence," pp. 551-552.

[63] *Personal Idealism and Mysticism,* 2nd ed. (London, 1913), p. 56.

[64] *The Platonic Tradition in English Religious Thought* (New York, 1926), p. 76.

[65] J. H. Muirhead, *The Platonic Tradition in Anglo-Saxon Philosophy* (London, 1931), p. 26. Gilson seems to be paraphrasing Shelley when he says "those all too uncertain truths which Greek speculation reserved for an intellectual elite, had already been brought together, purified, justified, completed by a revelation which put them within the reach of all the world." *Spirit of Mediaeval Philosophy* (London, 1936), p. 32.

[66] "Defence," p. 547.

we can lay these passages side by side with parallels in the earlier *Prometheus Unbound* and see that there is a difference. There it is lips that "enkindle"; and Asia is the Lucretian Venus, Nature—goddess, it is true, of Love and Beauty, "Child of Light," "*Life* of Life," "Lamp of Earth!"[67] The difference is largely one of emphasis. *Epipsychidion*, written just before the "Defence," concerns an amorous passion for a certain earthly woman, but here, even in celebrating "Free Love" (later changed to "True Love"), it is the light of Imagination which

> fills
> The Universe with glorious beams, and kills
> Error, the worm, with many a sun-like arrow
> Of its reverberated lightning. Narrow
> The heart that loves, the brain that contemplates,
> The life that wears, the spirit that creates
> One object, and one form, and builds thereby
> A sepulchre for its eternity.[68]

This is essentially his answer to Peacock's attack, which he read just before sending *Epipsychidion* off to the publisher, Ollier. Creative imagination and a range of spirit is needed; rationalism is not enough; life should not be pressed into *one form*. This is a protest against any kind of narrowness or dogmatism. In spite of his belief in the moral function of poetry, he can say with the deepest sincerity, "Didactic poetry is my abhorrence."[69] He wants his Prometheus—the spirit of Man —to be *unbound*. Hence the Socratic dialogue, not Aeschylus, is his avowed model.

Not metaphysical and logical "Dogma" but "Literature" is what Shelley aimed at—to use the terminology of Matthew Arnold's attack on religious and philosophical formulae. Like Shelley, Arnold was to offer poetry as a substitute for orthodox religion, making clear in a series of books and essays that by "poetry" he meant such works as the *Psalms, Isaiah,* and the religious literature of the Greeks—"a criticism of life." This is another manifestation of the Platonic identification of the true, the good, and the beautiful.

Shelley, later in his essay, defines "poetry in the universal sense" as the "forms of order and beauty according to which the materials of human life are susceptible of being arranged," and even "poetry in

---

[67] End of Act II. Italics mine. (II, v, 48 ff.)
[68] *Epipsychidion*, 166-173.
[69] Preface to *Prometheus Unbound*.

a restricted sense" has "a common source with all other forms of order and beauty."[70] In Plato's *Symposium*, as translated by Shelley (under the title of *The Banquet*), Diotima says poetry "is a general name signifying every cause whereby anything proceeds from that which is not, into that which is; so that the exercise of every inventive art is poetry, and all such artists poets. Yet they are not called poets, but distinguished by other names."[71] And Agathon has just said that everyone

becomes a poet as soon as he is touched by Love. . . . And who will deny that the divine poetry, by which all living things are produced upon the earth, is not [*sic*] harmonised by the wisdom of Love? Is it not evident that Love was the author of all the arts of life with which we are acquainted,

including, for example, medicine, archery, the loom, and the moulding of brass?[72] Shelley takes Agathon's speech seriously, and makes use of it in great passages in *Adonais*, though Plato was evidently holding up to ridicule its "detestable 'prose-poetry,' " and shows Agathon "not at all clear which Eros he is belauding, the 'heavenly' or the 'vulgar.' "[73] Nor is Shelley always clear. This is one way of identifying beauty and goodness that Plato did not mean to recommend. But Plato is voicing his own sober views in the *Laws* when he has the statesmen claim that they themselves

are tragic poets, and our tragedy is the best and noblest; for our whole state is an imitation of the best and noblest life. . . . You [makers of verses] are poets and we [statesmen] are poets, both makers of the same strains, rivals and antagonists in the noblest of dramas, which true law can alone perfect. . . . Wherefore, O ye sons and scions of the softer Muses, first of all show your songs to the magistrates, and let them compare them with our own, and if they are the same or better we will give you a chorus . . . .[74]

Likewise, Shelley says "religious and civil habits of action" by a figure of speech "may be called poetry"; and he speaks of poets as "those who imagine and express this indestructible order" of the true, good,

---

[70] "Defence," p. 567.

[71] Shelley, *Essays, Letters,* ed. Mrs. Shelley, I, 134. Also published "without change" in *Five Dialogues of Plato Bearing on Poetic Inspiration,* Everyman ed. (London, 1910), "Symposium," or "Banquet," trans. Shelley, section 205.

[72] *Ibid.,* I, 117. (Also in *Five Dialogues,* 196-197.)

[73] A. E. Taylor, *Plato, the Man and his Work* (New York, 1936), pp. 221-222. The same may be said of Browning, who got much of his philosophy from Shelley. See my "Introduction" to the Odyssey Press selections from Browning, *Pippa Passes and Shorter Poems* (New York, 1947).

[74] *Laws,* VII, 817.

and beautiful, including "the institutors of laws, and the founders of civil society. . . . Poets . . . were called, in the earlier epochs of the world, legislators or prophets."[75] This figure of speech by which in Plato's *Laws* the legislator claimed the poet's honors, is thus used with the reverse effect by Shelley, and points to the grand concluding sentence of his "Defence," "Poets are the unacknowledged legislators of the world"—his final answer to Peacock's—and Plato's—elevation of the art of government above the art of poetry.

Poetic Platonists have never been discouraged by Plato's attack on the poets, since Plato himself was such an encouraging example of "poet" in this most "universal" sense. And, indeed, in a more "restricted sense" not only the creation of the ideal republic which Plato terms a pattern laid up in heaven,[76] but also the great philosopher's literary art, his style, his power of characterization, the high intellectual comedy of his dialogue, his "myths," supply in Plato's own works an answer to any barren rationalism, even if it be that of Plato himself. How effective would Plato's theory of values have been if he had not recommended it with dramatic skill and poetic charm? As John Wild has said,

From the dialogues of Plato, we receive a living impression of the man Socrates, and our wills are stirred to that aspiration without which such knowledge [of universal truth] would never be achieved in the first place, nor ever applied to the actual lives of living men. . . . Contrary to a widespread misconception, it is only with a view to practice that theory achieves its most inclusive integration, *only in the light of the good* that all things can be seen in their proper station.

It is Plato's "essentially practical goal" that justifies "the use of analogy and myth, which have no place in the [Aristotelian] enterprise of pure understanding."[77] So the true pursuit of the good requires imaginative beauty.

---

[75] "Defence," pp. 533-534.

[76] *Republic*, IX, 592.

[77] John Wild, *Plato's Theory of Man, An Introduction to the Realistic Philosophy of Culture* (Cambridge, Mass., 1946), pp. 29-30, 32.

V. *Imagination; "Nous"; Imaginative Reason*

"Plato was essentially a poet," says Shelley, because of "the melody of his language," his ability "to kindle a harmony in thoughts," and "the truth and splendour of his imagery." Thus "the popular division into prose and verse is inadmissible," and "the distinction between poets and prose writers is a vulgar error."[78] We must keep this in mind when we find Shelley desiderating literary art as a *sine qua non* for our knowledge of the principles on which the social virtues are based. This may be illustrated by the very style in which Shelley says it: "What were virtue, love, patriotism, friendship . . . if poetry did not ascend to bring light and fire from those eternal regions where the owl-winged faculty of calculation dare not soar?"[79]

Shelley's emphasis is in line with the "neo-Platonic abandonment of Imitation, in favor of Imagination," referred to by Sikes:

Philostratus gave a new content to the term φαντασια: Pheidias and Praxiteles are not imitative but imaginative. . . . Plotinus settled the matter by his pronouncement that the arts "go back to the reasons from which nature comes; and further they create much out of themselves and add to that which is defective, as being themselves in possession of beauty." Plato's aesthetic was finally convicted by his own idealism.[80]

In "On the Symposium," Shelley mentions both the rational and the imaginative aspects of his master's mind:

Plato exhibits the rare union of close and subtle logic with the Pythian enthusiasm of poetry, melted by the splendour and harmony of his periods into one irresistible stream of musical impressions, which hurry the persuasions onward, as in a breathless career. . . . His excellence consists especially in intuition, and it is this faculty which raises him above Aristotle . . . .[81]

—though the latter's genius is also "vivid and various."

---

[78] "Defence," pp. 534-535.
[79] *Ibid.*, p. 561.
[80] *The Greek View of Poetry*, pp. 238-239.
[81] Shawcross, *op. cit.*, pp. 41-42.

Imagination does not merely create. What it perceives is real. Shelley carries this line of thought farther than most Platonists would. According to him, there is a *truth* of imagery. Even metaphor and rhythm are not arbitrary inventions; they discover something that was already there. (This view represents the opposite extreme from that which he sketched in his piece "On Life," that "Nothing exists but as it is perceived.")[82] Those in whom the

> faculty of approximation to the beautiful . . . exists in excess are poets, in the most universal sense of the word. . . . Their language is vitally metaphorical; that is, it marks the before unapprehended relations of things. . . . These similitudes or relations are finely said by Lord Bacon to be "the same footsteps of nature impressed upon the various subjects of the world" and he considers the faculty which perceives them as the storehouse of axioms common to all knowledge.[83]

And a few pages later Shelley recurs to this subject, designating three activities of poets: creative ("they are inventors"); metaphorical ("their words unveil the permanent analogy of things by images which participate in the life of truth"); and sensuous—and even in this third aspect poets are imitating something permanently real ("as their periods are harmonious and rhythmical, . . . being the echo of the eternal music.") In the very sentence from which these three passages have been quoted, Shelley is applying them to "all the authors of revolutions in opinion" to show that they are "necessarily poets." For example, "Lord Bacon was a poet." And on the other hand "Shakespeare, Dante, and Milton . . . are philosophers of the very loftiest power."[84] Here the Platonic tradition comes full circle. Plato banished the poets. Now Bacon, whose rationalistic utilitarianism is more extreme than that of Plato, is praised as a poet, and admitted to the company of the great philosopher Milton!

To create literature requires not merely *phantasia*, fancy, but what Plato himself called *nous*, which we can now, following Coleridge's distinction, translate *reason*. But Shelley often used the word "reason" for "the owl-winged faculty of calculation" that Coleridge labeled mere "understanding." Shelley was following eighteenth-century terminology, Coleridge reviving a Renaissance concept. Michael Roberts has shown that in some ways

the history of English and French philosophy in the eighteenth century is,

---

[82] *Ibid.*, p. 56, dated 1815 by Shawcross.
[83] "Defence," p. 532.
[84] *Ibid.*, p. 536.

in the main, the history of the gradual restriction of the concept of reason. And at the same time, because some name must be used for that which is felt to exist, it is the history of the growth and widening of the concept of 'imagination.'

Reason had been regarded as man's highest faculty at a time when it meant right judgment and the use of every kind of awareness. It was still regarded as man's highest faculty, though now its meaning had been narrowed down to the recognition of plain material facts and matter-of-fact logic. Something which had been necessary to make it worthy of such respect had evaporated. . . . The something which had evaporated, Coleridge proposed to call 'imagination'[85]

—and so did Shelley. But "to Coleridge, knowledge and truth and reason still meant a capacity for right judgment and for decisions involving the whole man." The best solution of the terminological conflict was perhaps Matthew Arnold's fusion of the terms into the phrase "imaginative reason." That is the Platonic *nous*.

It is the mere Coleridgean "understanding" Shelley means when, in the first paragraph of his "Defence," he writes concerning the "principle of analysis": "Reason is the enumeration of quantities already known; imagination is the perception of the value of those quantities, both separately and as a whole. Reason respects the differences, and imagination the similitudes of things." Noteworthy indeed is his assumption that the imagination, too, is cognitive, is a means of knowing.

And Shelley was not always willing to cede the word *reason* to the rationalists. With the Bodleian manuscript sources of "A Defence of Poetry," Mr. A. H. Koszul found and printed fragments from a translation by Shelley of a passage from Plato's *Ion* that is used in the "Defence." It is remarkable that in this translation Shelley manages to avoid saying what his fuller published translation of the *Ion* says, that the poets are like those "who lose all control over their reason" and that the poet cannot compose "whilst any reason remains in him." E.g., for the latter he substitutes "until understanding be no longer in him."[86] And in an addition to his Proposed Letter to Ollier, the Editor of the *Literary Miscellany*, Shelley wrote of Peacock, "He would extinguish Imagination which is the Sun of life, and grope his way by the cold and uncertain and borrowed light of that moon *which he calls* Reason, stumbling over the interlunar chasm of time where she deserts us . . . ." (Italics mine.)

---

[85] Michael Roberts, *The Modern Mind* (London, 1937), pp. 123, 139.

[86] Koszul, *op. cit.*, p. 121; Shelley's translation of the *Ion* in *Essays, Letters*, ed. Mrs. Shelley, I, 282, 283. (Also in *Five Dialogues*, section 534).

"But let us *in true sense* place within the scan of reason an opinion so light . . . ."[87]

Nevertheless, when he came to write his "Defence" he allowed Peacock's eighteenth-century, or *philosophe*, meaning for the term *reason*, and thus planted in his essay a fruitful source of misinterpretation, tempting us to think it more romantic, less Platonic, than it really is.

---

[87] Koszul, *op. cit.*, pp. 119-120.

VI. *Knowledge the Key to Virtue*

Does Shelley, like Plato, treat knowledge as the key to virtue? Professor Ellsworth Barnard has interpreted Shelley closer to Christianity than was ever done before; and in this respect that means farther from Plato. In his Odyssey Press selections from Shelley, Barnard declares that a doctrine which "rests on the fundamental Platonic teaching that men always err involuntarily, through ignorance alone, is inconsistent with the main tendency of Shelley's thought. Over and over Shelley tells us that . . . human beings suffer because, knowing the better, they choose the worse." Nevertheless, Professor Barnard admits that he finds this Platonic doctrine in the "Defence" and in the Preface to *The Cenci*.[88] Barnard's note is attached to that passage in the "Defence" which states that in Athenian tragedy the "imagination is enlarged by a sympathy with pains and passions so mighty, that they distend in their conception the capacity of that by which they are conceived; the good affections are strengthened by pity, indignation, terror, and sorrow"— in this clause Shelley is in agreement with neither Plato nor with Aristotle's answer to Plato, on tragedy—and crime loses

its contagion by being represented as the fatal consequence of the unfathomable agencies of nature; error is thus divested of its wilfulness; men can no longer cherish it as the creation of their choice. In a drama of the highest order there is little food for censure or hatred; it teaches rather self-knowledge and self-respect.[89]

The kind of knowledge which does not produce virtue, and the way in which knowledge, through poetry, does develop virtue, are made clear in another passage which first dismisses as ineffective the schemes propounded by "ethical science," adding,

---

[88] Cf. "The highest moral purpose aimed at in the highest species of the drama, is the teaching of the human heart, through its sympathies and antipathies, the knowledge of itself; in proportion to the possession of which knowledge, every human being is wise, just, sincere, tolerant, and kind." Preface, *Cenci*, p. 196 of Barnard's *Shelley* in the Odyssey Press Series.

[89] "Defence," p. 544.

nor is it for want of admirable doctrines that men hate, and despise, and censure, and deceive, and subjugate one another. But poetry acts in another and a diviner manner. It awakens and enlarges the mind itself by rendering it the receptacle of a thousand unapprehended combinations of thought. . . . A man, to be greatly good, must imagine intensely and comprehensively; he must put himself in the place of another and of many others; the pains and pleasures of his species must become his own. The great instrument of moral good is the imagination.[90]

This is an eloquent defense of the moral and social value of the knowledge offered by the humanities, particularly in the Classical tradition. That tradition is often more relevant for the interpretation of "A Defence of Poetry" than Shelley's own lyrical reaction to personal experiences. His lyrics may make us suspect that he was not perfect in self-knowledge. But the heart of his essay is the Platonic conviction that the good life is to be derived from knowledge of self and of universal values.

---

[90] *Ibid.*, pp. 539-540.

VII. *Reminiscence; Intuition of Eternal Ideas*

One of the first things that interested Shelley in Plato was evidently the doctrine of Reminiscence, referred to in the *Phaedo* as a conception which Socrates is "frequently accustomed to employ," namely, "that knowledge is simply recollection."[91] The doctrine of Reminiscence or Recollection (*anamnésis*) is set forth by Socrates in Plato's *Meno:*

> The soul, then, as being immortal, and having been born again many times, and having seen all things that exist, whether in this world or in the world below, has knowledge of them all; and it is no wonder that she should be able to call to remembrance all that she ever knew about virtue and about everything . . . for all enquiry and all learning is but recollection.[92]

What A. E. Taylor says of Plato at this point could be said of Shelley's "Defence": "The main emphasis thus falls not on the Orphic doctrine of pre-existence and re-incarnation," but rather on "the function of sense-experience as suggestive of and pregnant with truths of an intelligible order which it does not itself adequately embody or establish."[93]

In *Queen Mab* (finished in 1813) Shelley writes:

> For birth but wakes the spirit to the sense
> Of outward shows, whose unexperienced shape
> New modes of passion to its frame may lend;

In *The Daemon of the World,* two or three years later, this was revised to:

> For birth but wakes the universal mind
> Whose mighty streams might else in silence flow

---

[91] *Phaedo,* section 72E. Though the last clause is from Jowett, the first quoted phrase is from Thomas Taylor's translation, more accurate than Jowett's "Your favourite doctrine." Cebes says, "kat' ekeinon ge ton logon O Socrates, ei alēthēs estin, hon su eiōthas thama legein, hoti hēmin hē mathēsis ouk allo ti ē anam-nēsis tugchanei ousa . . ." Taylor's translation uses the word *reminiscence* and continues: "according to this, it is necessary that we must have learned the things which we now call to mind in some former period of time. But this is impossible, unless our soul subsisted somewhere before it took up its residence in this human form." (Taylor, *Works of Plato* [London, 1804], IV, 281-282).

[92] Section 81, Jowett tr.

[93] *Plato,* p. 136.

Thro' the vast world, to individual sense
Of outward shows.[94]

Comparing these two versions, we can observe Shelley's rapid development, after *Queen Mab,* toward more philosophical thinking. But at this point he seems to speak more as a Pantheist than as a Platonist. The bridge between the two is, logically, Neo-Platonism; and Shelley is often on that bridge, as we shall note later.

There is nothing philosophical in one of the incidents which shows Shelley's early interest in Plato. While he was in college he stopped a woman with a baby and asked her if her baby would tell anything about pre-existence, adding, "How provokingly close are those new born babes . . . but it is not the less certain, notwithstanding the cunning attempts to conceal the truth, that all knowledge is reminiscence: the Doctrine is far more ancient than the times of Plato."[95]

In the "Defence" there are echoes of Reminiscence, more mature and subtle: In poetry, "a word, a trait . . . will touch the enchanted chord, and reanimate, in those who have ever experienced these emotions, the sleeping, the cold, the buried image of the past. . . . Poetry redeems from decay the visitations of the divinity in man." It "purges from our inward sight the film of familiarity which obscures from us the wonder of our being. . . . It creates anew the universe, after it has been annihilated in our minds by the recurrence of impressions blunted by reiteration."[96] This suggests Plato's *Phaedrus,* especially Socrates' account of the experience of each soul when it has ascended—soared—into those eternal regions where

the intelligence of every soul which is capable of receiving the food proper to it, rejoices at beholding reality, and once more gazing upon truth, is replenished and made glad, until the revolution of the worlds brings her round again to the same place. In the revolution she beholds justice, and temperance, and knowledge absolute. . . . But when she is unable to follow, and fails to behold the truth, and through some ill-hap sinks beneath the double load of forgetfulness and vice, and her wings fall from her and she drops to the ground, then the law ordains that this soul shall at her first birth pass, not into any other animal, but only into man. . . . But the soul which has never seen the truth will not pass into the human form. For a man must have intelligence of universals, and be able to proceed from the many particulars of sense to one conception of reason;—this is the recollection of those things which our soul once saw while following God—when regardless of that which we now call being she raised her

---

94 "Queen Mab," IX, 155-157; "The Daemon of the World," 539.
95 White, *Shelley,* I, 84-85.
96 "Defence," pp. 563-564.

head up towards the true being. . . . And he who employs aright these memories is ever being initiated into perfect mysteries and alone becomes truly perfect. But, as he forgets earthly interests and is rapt in the divine, the vulgar deem him mad, and rebuke him; they do not see that he is inspired. Thus far I have been speaking of the fourth and last kind of madness, which is imputed to him who, when he sees the beauty of earth, is transported with the recollection of the true beauty; he would like to fly away, but he cannot; he is like a bird fluttering and looking upward and careless of the world below; and he is therefore thought to be mad. And I have shown this of all inspirations to be the noblest and highest . . . to him who has or shares it. . . . But all souls do not easily recall the things of the other world. . . . Few only retain an adequate remembrance of them; and they, when they behold here any image of that other world, are rapt in amazement . . . .[97]

This passage suggests Shelley's "To a Skylark," "Hymn to Intellectual Beauty," and the reference to himself as "A herd-abandoned deer" who "Had gazed on Nature's naked loveliness."[98] It would supply him with a justification of himself, as poet.

Shelley passes from the crude doctrine of pre-existence, "memories of an antenatal life," in *Prince Athanase* (1817—line 91) to a more philosophic concern with the perception of "those first principles which belong to the imagination"—"the *eternal truths charactered upon the imaginations* of men."[99] In this respect, even Peacock's attack on poetry admits the Platonic claim, for he says, "It is only the more tangible points of morality, those which command assent at once, those which *have a mirror in every mind* . . . that are applicable even to what is called moral poetry," and this state of mind, in which there is a mixture of reason, feeling, and imagination, Peacock contrasts with "dispassionate reasoning,"[100] what Shelley calls "an unmitigated exercise of the calculating faculty"—Coleridge's "Understanding."

We have seen how, in Shelley's view, poetry "enlarges the mind" with intuitive knowledge. But notice the doctrine of Reminiscence implied, especially in the portion of his statement I here underline:

It awakens and enlarges the mind. . . . Poetry lifts the veil from the hidden beauty of the world . . . it *re*-produces all that it represents, and the impersonations clothed in its Elysian light stand thenceforward in the minds of those who have contemplated them, as memorials of that gentle

---

[97] *Phaedrus*, trans. Jowett, 247-250.
[98] "Adonais," 297, 275.
[99] "Defence," p. 558. (Italics mine, here and in the two following quotations.)
[100] *Four Ages*, p. 52.

[34]

and exalted content which extends itself over all thoughts and actions with which it co-exists.[101]

This beauty is not always placed in the temporal past or future and spatially in another location; rather it is the true reality of what is eternally present. "The imagination beholding the beauty of this order, created it out of itself according to its own idea,"[102] as one may behold the pattern of the ideal Republic, Plato tells us, "and beholding, may set his own house in order."[103] As a matter of fact, this statement by Shelley continues, "the consequence was empire," and he is referring to Rome, for "The true poetry of Rome lived in its institutions; for whatever of beautiful, true, and majestic, they contained, could have sprung only from the faculty which creates the order in which they consist."[104] In order to say this, he had to shut his eyes to much that is ugly in the history of Rome. And he must have known he was falsifying the picture. In the manuscript he had written:

But the beauty & the excellence of that system of civil society which terminated in the overthrow of the liberties of the world and of its own; and which is even now the basis of those systems of tyranny to which its barbarian destroyers have conformed, can scarcely be produced in competition with Poetry the source of whatever beauty or excellence of which any [form] or institution or opinion is susceptible.[105]

This is what turned into praise of empire in his final text! In this alteration I think we hear the falsetto note that sometimes disturbs us in Shelley's rendering of the eternal music. So easily does Platonic idealism seeking "the very image of life expressed in its eternal truth"[106] slip over into a romantic idealism which "adds beauty to that which is most deformed." He manages, indeed, to offer both in one compound clause, speaking of the power of poetry to create, "whether it spreads its own figured curtain, or withdraws life's dark veil from before the scene of things."[107] But his own theoretical interest is in the Platonic truth, not the romantic illusions, of imaginative art. Whether or not Rome illustrates his point, he is in agreement with Plato when he claims that orderly institutions are created by a mind inspired by love and in accord with eternal ideas.

---

[101] "Defence," pp. 539-540. I have taken "re-produces" from the MS. reading, instead of "reproduces," which now fails to convey the evident meaning. See Koszul, *op. cit.*, p. 77.

[102] *Ibid.*, p. 549.

[103] *Republic*, IX, 592B.

[104] "Defence," p. 549.

[105] Koszul, *op. cit.*, p. 90.

[106] "Defence," p. 536.

[107] *Ibid.*, p. 564.

VIII. *Participation in Ideal Forms*

On the subject of Reminiscence, the significant contribution of Plato to Shelley's thought is not merely the doctrine of the pre-existence of the soul, as in Wordsworth's "Intimations of Immortality," but rather a recognition that man's true home is in the realm of ideas or ideal forms. So he says that Keats, in dying, "Hath awakened from the dream of life." The weapon of the spirit is of the eternal world; shall it "Be as a sword consumed before the sheath," i.e., cease to exist even before the material of the "leprous corpse" disappears? Keats has outsoared "Envy and calumny and hate and pain." " 'Tis we, who, lost in stormy visions," strike "invulnerable nothings" with the spirit's knife—as in this very poem "Adonais," where the "spirit's knife" was striking at the false reviewers who had failed to appreciate Keats and Shelley. To fight with such "nothings" was a "mad trance"; they remained invulnerable. While we are not yet released from material existence,

> *We* decay
> Like corpses in a charnel; fear and grief
> Convulse us and consume us day by day,
> And cold hopes swarm like worms within our living clay.[108]

This is both a lyric outcry from Shelley's tortured experience, and an expression of Platonic doctrine from the *Phaedo:* "that while we are in the body, and while the soul is infected with the evils of the body, our desire will not be satisfied," but in death "having got rid of the foolishness of the body we shall be pure and hold converse with the pure, and know of ourselves the clear light everywhere, which is no other than the light of truth."[109]

In Shelley's faith, if history does not adequately shadow forth the earthly course of the Ideal City, then so much the worse

> For this keen-judging world, this two-edged lie,
> Which seems, but is not.

---

108 "Adonais," 178, 343-353.
109 *Phaedo*, trans. Jowett, 66-67.

> this familiar life, which seems to be
> But is not—or is but quaint mockery
> Of all we would believe

> Life, like a dome of many-coloured glass,
> Stains the white radiance of Eternity,
> Until Death tramples it to fragments.—Die,
> If thou wouldst be with that which thou dost seek![110]

The stanza from which these last four lines are taken begins with the declaration that "The One remains, the many change and pass"; which may well remind us that "A poet participates in the eternal, the infinite, and the one; as far as relates to his conceptions, time and place and number are not."[111] His interest is in the universal, the ideal forms in the realm of ideas. Poetry "makes us the inhabitants of a world to which the familiar world is a chaos,"[112]

> in this life
> Of error, ignorance, and strife,
> Where nothing is, but all things seem,
>   . . . . . .
> For love, and beauty, and delight,
> There is no death nor change . . .[113]

"There is nothing new," says Socrates, "in what I am about to tell you; but only what I have been always and everywhere repeating . . . for I cannot help thinking, if there be anything beautiful other than absolute beauty . . . that it can be beautiful only in so far as it partakes of absolute beauty . . . assured in my own mind that nothing makes a thing beautiful but the presence and participation of beauty. . . ."[114] Shelley, in 1816, hailed the

> Spirit of Beauty, that dost consecrate
>   With thine own hues all thou dost shine upon . . . .
>   . . . . . .
> Thou—that to human thought art nourishment
>   . . . . . .
>   Sudden, thy shadow fell on me;
>   I shrieked, and clasped my hands in ecstasy![115]

---

[110] *The Cenci* (1819), IV, i, 115-116; "Letter to Maria Gisborne" (1820), 156-158; "Adonais" (1821), 462-465.
[111] "Defence," p. 533.
[112] *Ibid.*, p. 564.
[113] "The Sensitive Plant" (1820), 122-124, 134-135.
[114] *Phaedo*, 100.
[115] "Hymn to Intellectual Beauty," 13-14, 44, 59-60.

In the *Phaedrus* we read that

The divine is beauty, wisdom, goodness, and the like; and by these the wing of the soul is nourished.

But of beauty, I repeat again that we saw her there shining in company with the celestial forms; and coming to earth we find her here too, shining in clearness through the clearest aperture of sense. For sight is the most piercing of our bodily senses; though not by that is wisdom seen; her loveliness would have been transporting if there had been a visible image of her, and the other ideas, if they had visible counterparts, would be equally lovely. . . .

He whose initiation is recent, and who has been the spectator of many glories in the other world, is amazed when he sees any one having a godlike face or form, which is the expression of divine beauty; and at first a shudder runs through him, and again the old awe steals over him. . . .[116]

There are Platonic echoes in Shelley's reference to "evanescent visitations of thought and feeling" which are "elevating and delightful beyond all expression" that leave behind "pleasure, participating as it does in the nature of its object . . . its footsteps are like those of a wind over the sea, which the coming calm erases. . . ." This is "experienced principally by those of the most delicate sensibility" and the "state of mind" thus produced "is at war with every base desire."[117] Shelley's language will suggest at one moment Platonic Forms, at the next moment a mystical Spirit; and he blurs the distinction between Love and Beauty. He is, as it were, more Greek than Plato as a worshipper of the Uranian Aphrodite (Love, Intellectual Beauty), a God of whom he says "she sped" through

> human hearts, which to her aery tread
> Yielding not, wounded the invisible
> Palms of her tender feet where'er they fell:
> And barbed tongues, and thoughts more sharp then they,
> Rent the soft Form they never could repel[118]

This, and the similar allusions in the "Defence," are surely echoes of Plato's *Symposium,* from that same speech of Agathon's which we have quoted concerning the wisdom of Love, "author of all the arts of life":

Love walks not upon the earth, nor over the heads of men, which are not indeed very soft, but he dwells within, and treads on the softest of existing things, having established his habitation within the souls and inmost nature

---

[116] *Phaedrus,* 246, 250, 251.
[117] "Defence," p. 563.
[118] "Adonais," 210-214.

of gods and men; not indeed in all souls—for wherever he chances to find a hard and rugged disposition there he will not inhabit, but only where it is most soft and tender . . . His life is spent among flowers . . . the winged Love rests not in his flight . . . within any soul the flower of whose loveliness is faded . . . Love is a great poet.[119]

And this god who "is a wise poet" is "the youngest and the most delicate of all divinities." That is indeed Shelley's conception of the Poet as a "frail Form," a "gentle child,"

> a portion of the loveliness
> Which once he made more lovely[120]

We usually find the wisdom of Plato in the words he puts into the mouth of Socrates; but Shelley's Plato was Agathon too!

---

[119] "The Banquet," trans. Shelley, in *Essays, Letters,* ed. Mrs. Shelley, I, 114, 115, 117.

[120] "Adonais," 271, 235, 379-380. Cf. "Defence," p. 552, "becoming a portion of that beauty which we contemplate."

IX. *Hostility to Imitation of Phenomena*

Like Plato and Aristotle, Shelley objects to a "story of particular facts," but unlike Plato he considers this no objection to poetry. Thus he makes the usual Platonist correction of Plato: Poetry is not photographic (or phonographic) imitation of the visible and audible world that impinges on our senses. Poetry does not reproduce what John Crowe Ransom calls "the world's body" (in a book of that title), or what Prall calls "aesthetic surface."[121] Rather:

A poem is the very image of life expressed in its eternal truth. There is this difference between a story and a poem, that a story is a catalogue of detached facts, which have no other bond of connexion than time, place, circumstance, cause, and effect; the other is the creation of actions according to the unchangeable forms of human nature.[122]

It is, he says, "universal." Here Shelley is in agreement with Aristotle's emphasis on probability, on the normal humanity of the tragic hero, who is best conceived of as "like us," and especially on the distinction between poetry and history. But Shelley very quickly departs from Aristotle, moving in the direction exemplified by John Henry Newman in his essay on Aristotle's *Poetics* eight years later, where Newman was to set forth the view that poetry

delineates that perfection which the imagination suggests, and to which as a limit the present system of Divine Providence actually tends . . . it recreates the imagination by the superhuman loveliness of its views, it provides a solace for the mind broken by the disappointments and sufferings of actual life.[123]

---

[121] D. W. Prall, *Aesthetic Analysis* (New York, 1936). See my article, "Aesthetic Surface in the Novel," *The Trollopian* (Sept., 1947).

[122] "Defence," pp. 536-537.

[123] When Newman wrote this, Shelley's "Defence of Poetry" had not been published. See the comparison of Newman, Shelley, and Aristotle in Alvan Ryan's "Newman's Conception of Literature," in *Critical Studies in Arnold, Emerson, and Newman* (Iowa City, 1942), pp. 129-131, 173. Most astonishing is the fact that Newman ascribes this ultra-romantic view to Aristotle's *Poetics*.

Shelley is not quite so romantic as this, but he declares that "Homer embodied the ideal perfection of his age in human character. . . . Nor let it be objected, that these characters are remote from moral perfection," for "a poet considers the vices of his contemporaries as a temporary dress in which his creations must be arrayed, and which cover without concealing the eternal proportions of their beauty."[124] Likewise, "The distorted notions of invisible things which Dante and his rival Milton have idealized, are merely the mask and the mantle in which these great poets walk through eternity enveloped and disguised." At this point the essay omits a sentence which Shelley had written in his manuscript—"Let us refrain from a discussion [of] the origins of those monstrous opinions which Dante & Milton idealized which involves no less than an inquiry into the origin of evil."[125] (So Shelley described himself as "A Love in desolation masked.")[126] Tragedy does not aim at an effect of horror; rather, by it "crime is disarmed of half its horror," and "The tragedies of the Athenian poets are as mirrors in which the spectator beholds himself, under a thin disguise of circumstance, stript of all but that ideal perfection and energy which every one feels to be the internal type of all that he loves, admires, and would become."[127] It would seem incredible that Shelley could say this if he had ever read, say, *Philoctetes*. But it happens that he has just mentioned Philoctetes—and also Agamemnon and Othello—in a passage found cancelled in the manuscript.[128] The kind of "idealism" represented in these passages from Newman and Shelley is certainly romantic rather than Platonic. In contrast, Sir Philip Sidney after mentioning the virtues of Achilles and Ulysses (mentioned also by Shelley), went on to cite,

contrarily . . . the soon-repenting pride of Agamemnon; the self-devouring cruelty in his father Atreus, the violence of ambition in the two Theban brothers; the sour sweetness of revenge in Medea . . . and finally, all virtues, vices, and passions so in their own natural states laid to the view, that we seem not to hear of them, but clearly to see through them.

Sidney's is at this point the more genuinely Platonic defence of the poet's relation to the "many infallible grounds of wisdom, which not-

---

[124] "Defence," pp. 538-539.
[125] *Ibid.*, p. 553; and Koszul, *op. cit.*, p. 97.
[126] "Adonais," 281.
[127] "Defence," pp. 543-544.
[128] Koszul, *op. cit.*, p. 82.

withstanding lie dark before the imaginative and judging power, if they be not illuminated or figured forth by the speaking picture of poesy."[129] But it must be obvious that Sidney's argument is much closer to Shelley than to Plato, who never recognized, in theory, the natural affinity between literary art and his own type of idealism.

A Rousseauistic faith in the natural goodness of man is evident in Shelley's early writings; e.g. at the end of the long note to *Queen Mab,* V, he wrote:

> That which will result from the abolition of marriage will be natural and right; because choice and change will be exempted from restraint. In fact, religion and morality, as they now stand, compose a practical code of misery and servitude: the genius of human happiness must tear every leaf from the accursed book of God ere man can read the inscription on his heart.

If social and moral evils (like "Revenge" and "Self-deceit") are merely "a temporary dress" and such clothing includes conventions and institutions, then all we need is that our Sartor should be *"resartus."* The similarity between the apparent anarchist Shelley and the pre-fascist Carlyle should not be ignored. Whatever either may think of the common man (and neither is entirely consistent), at least of epic and dramatic heroes Shelley declares: "The beauty of the internal nature can not be so far concealed by its accidental vesture, but that the spirit of its form shall communicate itself to the very disguise."[130] But there is a Platonic germ to Shelley's conception that the *real* man is good, in spite of

> self-loved ignorance,
> Or other such foul masks, with which ill thoughts
> Hide that fair being whom we spirits call man;[131]

The idea that human souls as they enter earthly life "through birth's orient portal" in effect "clothe themselves in matter," runs through Plato's *Phaedo,* though these phrases are from Shelley.[132]

And if the visible world is not the true home that man should seek, it is not surprising that Plato objects to the artist's holding the mirror up to nature, creating untrue appearances as if by "turning a mirror round and round," to use Plato's comparison from the *Republic.*[133] Shel-

---

[129] Sidney, *Apology,* pp. 16-17.

[130] "Defence," p. 539.

[131] *Prometheus Unbound,* III, iv, 43-45.

[132] "Hellas" (1821), 202, and Shelley's note to that chorus. Shelley in this chorus also suggests reincarnation, apparently in accord with the *Phaedrus* and the "Vision of Er" in the *Republic,* X.

[133] *Republic,* X, 596.

ley, however, admires the drama, "as a prismatic and many-sided mirror, which collects the brightest rays of human nature and divides and reproduces them from the simplicity of these elementary forms, and touches them with majesty and beauty, and multiplies all that it reflects."[134] This mirror would seem very much like a dome of prismatic glass, which beautifies rather than stains the white radiance of eternal human nature. Like other Platonists, Shelley thus shows himself less ready than Plato to condemn the drama for its mirroring; he considered it an imitation not of transient phenomena but of Platonic "elementary forms."

Thus "Poetry turns all things to loveliness" not only when "it adds beauty to that which is most deformed"—a process admired by Shelley but antipathetic to the very spirit of Platonism—but in a more profound sense, deeply Platonic:

It transmutes all that it touches, and every form moving within the radiance of its presence is changed by wondrous sympathy to an incarnation of the spirit which it breathes; its secret alchemy turning to potable gold the poisonous waters which flow from death through life; it strips the veil of familiarity from the world, and lays bare the naked and sleeping beauty, which is the spirit of its forms . . . poetry defeats the curse which binds us to be subjected to the accident of surrounding impressions.[135]

Likewise to the eyes of the Witch of Atlas

> The naked beauty of the soul lay bare,
> And often through a rude and worn disguise
> She saw the inner form most bright and fair—[136]

If to some extent we may take this Witch to be, as E. E. Kellet argues, a personification of the creative imagination, or let us say, poetry (which to Shelley meant the same thing) and one of the manifestations of Intellectual Beauty, the following is close to the Platonism of the "Defence":

> her beauty made
> The bright world dim, and everything beside
> Seemed like the fleeting image of a shade:
> . . . . . .
> Which when the lady knew, she took her spindle
> . . . . . .
> And with these threads a subtle veil she wove—
> A shadow for the splendour of her love.[137]

---

134 "Defence," p. 544.
135 *Ibid.*, p. 564.
136 "The Witch of Atlas" (1820), 572-573.
137 *Ibid.*, 137-152.

Likewise in the "Defence" Shelley asserts: "Few poets of the highest class have chosen to exhibit the beauty of their conceptions in its naked truth and splendour; and it is doubtful whether the alloy of costume, habit, &c., be not necessary to temper this planetary music for mortal ears."[138] This is similar to what Plato says in the *Phaedrus* concerning Wisdom (rather than Beauty—but the transfer is easy for a Platonist): she is not perceived with the senses, for "her loveliness would have been transporting if there had been a visible image of her." So such "ideas" do not have "visible counterparts" but remain "planetary."[139] In "Adonais" Shelley represents himself as having suffered the pain of one who "Had gazed on Nature's naked loveliness, Actaeon-like." And in a Sonnet of 1818 he wrote:

> Lift not the painted veil which those who live
> Call Life: tho' unreal shapes be pictured there,
> And it but mimic all we would believe
> With colors idly spread,—behind, lurk Fear
> And Hope, twin destinies. . . .
> I knew one who had lifted it—he sought,
>   . . . things to love,
> But found them not, alas! nor was there aught
> The world contains, the which he could approve.
> Thro' the unheeding many he did move,
> A splendor among shadows, a bright blot
> Upon this gloomy scene, a Spirit that strove
> For truth, and like the Preacher found it not.

But later under the tutelage of Plato he was to find behind the unreal shapes of life "things to love" and truth so dazzling that perhaps its beauty must be veiled to mortals. Here we reach a curious paradox: In spite of all the power of poetry to utter the ineffable, one of the advantages of poetry is just that the

> beams of brightest verse
> Are clouds to hide, not colours to portray . . .[140]

Shelley was awakened to *intellectual* Beauty—yet this was through the sensuousness of the "sweet time when winds are wooing." Beauty's *light* is "like mist" and manifests itself as a *shadow*—and this shadow itself "Floats though unseen among us."[141] Of course these inconsistencies

---

138 "Defence," p. 539.
139 *Phaedrus,* 250. Quoted in context, above.
140 *Prometheus Unbound,* IV, 534-535.
141 "Hymn to Intellectual Beauty," 55-56, 32, 1-2.

can be dismissed as illogical phrasing; but we need not do so. We should consider the difficulty of stating in any one critical formula the relation between universals and aesthetic reality. In Shelley's poetry, we are often confronted with romantic suggestiveness rather than clear presentation. But the "Defence" is an attempt to answer, philosophically, a utilitarian attack on poetry, especially on romantic poetry; hence in the essay Shelley stresses the usefulness of literary beauty, its success in attaining and communicating that virtuous knowledge which Plato himself had assigned pre-eminently to philosophers.[142] Coming from Shelley's poetry to his "Defence," one may be surprised to find how closely the latter resembles the Renaissance reasoning of Sir Philip Sidney. The poet "showeth himself a passionate lover of that unspeakable and everlasting beauty to be seen by the eyes of the mind," not "captived to the truth of a foolish world."[143] In neither Plato nor Shelley do we find any praise for naturalistic realism, the "imitation of appearances."[144]

---

[142] But Socrates says (*Phaedrus*, 278) that poets are worthy to be called philosophers "if their compositions are based on knowledge of the truth," and if they can defend them "by spoken arguments."

[143] Sidney, *Apology*, pp. 6, 21.

[144] Plato, *Republic*, X, especially 598B.

X. *The Poet's Irrational Inspiration*

Socrates concluded that

not by wisdom [*sophia*] do poets write poetry, but by a sort of genius [*phusei*] and inspiration [*enthousiazontes*]; they are like diviners or soothsayers [*hoi theomanteis kai hoi chrēsmōdoi*] who also say many fine things, but do not understand the meaning of them . . . and I further observed that upon the strength of their poetry they believed themselves to be the wisest of men in other things in which they were not wise.[145]

The latter part of this passage might have embarrassed Shelley, if he had been capable of being embarrassed. Actually he answers Socrates roundly, "That he [the poet] is the wisest [of men] . . . is . . . incontrovertible." But he would certainly agree with the first part of Socrates' statement, if we take *sophia* as meaning not Holy Wisdom but rather the "science" which *sophists* pretended to teach. This is one of the most important tenets of Socrates: that the poet is divinely inspired, like a prophet. Shelley says "a poet essentially comprises" the character of prophet (as well as legislator).[146] In *Prometheus Unbound*,

> the harmonious mind
> Poured itself forth in all-prophetic song[147]

The "poet participates in the divine nature."[148] Shelley's Apollo is not only the god to whom bards hold fealty; he is in that very fact the god of "all prophecy," and declares,

> I am the eye with which the Universe
> Beholds itself and knows itself divine;[149]

---

[145] Plato, *Apology of Socrates*, 22C, using Jowett's English; note the reference to a *theos* (god) in two of the words I have added in Greek.
[146] "Defence," pp. 563, 533.
[147] *Prometheus*, II, iv, 75-76.
[148] "Defence," p. 546.
[149] "Hymn of Apollo," 31 ff.

In the critical thought of the Romantic era, the conception of "the poet as prophet" was common. Indeed, this phrase in its broadest sense may serve to designate what has always been one of the most important ways of recognizing the social function of serious literature. But Plato and Shelley carry this farther than some others do. A typical Renaissance critic, Sir Philip Sidney, treats the poet as moral teacher and mentions that "among the Romans a poet was called *vates*, which is as much a diviner, foreseer, or prophet. . . . And may not I presume a little further to show the reasonableness of this word *vates*, and say that the holy David's Psalms are a divine poem?"[150] But Sidney will not go the full length with Plato, "since he attributeth unto poesy more than myself do, namely to be a very inspiring of a divine force, far above man's wit."[151] But Shelley is willing to go the full distance: Poetry is "the interpenetration of a diviner nature through our own." And when at a crucial place in his "Defence," he turns from answering Peacock to making a positive claim, he says, "Poetry is indeed something divine,"[152] echoing Plato's *Ion*, as translated by Shelley himself: "poems are not human as the work of men, but divine as coming from God."[153] (Shelley does not accept the next point made by Socrates, that "the God designedly inspires the worst poets with the sublimest verse.")

We could think of an inspiration as something rational, from a Divine *Logos*, "the true Light" of a Universal Reason. But in both Plato and Shelley the view that poetic creation is inspired is associated with the view that it is irrational. In the *Phaedrus*, Socrates subdivides "divine madness" into "four kinds, prophetic, initiatory, poetic, erotic." Shelley fuses three of these: the first, "the inspiration of Apollo . . . the third that of the Muses, the fourth that of Aphrodite and Eros," ignoring "the second that of Dionysus." Any of these forms of madness, says Socrates, is "a divine release of the soul from the yoke of custom and convention."[154] (That must have delighted Shelley.) Of these,

The third kind is the madness of those who are possessed by the Muses; which taking hold of a delicate and virgin soul, and there inspiring frenzy, awakens lyrical and all other numbers. . . . But he who, having no touch of the Muses' madness in his soul, comes to the door and thinks that he will get into the temple by the help of art [*technes*, professional technique]—

---

[150] Sidney, *Apology*, pp. 5-6.
[151] *Ibid.*, p. 43.
[152] "Defence," pp. 563, 561.
[153] *Ion*, 534, (*Essays, Letters*, ed. Mrs. Shelley, I, 284).
[154] *Phaedrus*, p. 265.

he, I say, and his poetry are not admitted; the sane man disappears and is nowhere when he enters into rivalry with the madman.[155]

Shelley wrote to Peacock, August 16, 1818, "What a wonderful passage there is in *Phaedrus*—the beginning, I think, of one of the speeches of Socrates—in praise of poetic madness, and in definition of what poetry is, and how a man becomes a poet."[156] In his "Defence," three years later he writes:

Poetry, as has been said, differs in this respect from logic, that it is not subject to the control of the active powers of the mind, and that its birth and recurrence have no necessary connexion with consciousness or will.

Poetry is not like reasoning, a power to be exerted according to the determination of the will . . . for the mind in creation is as a fading coal, which some invisible influence, like an inconstant wind, awakens to transitory brightness . . . I appeal to the greatest poets of the present day, whether it be not an error to assert that the finest passages of poetry are produced by labour and study.[157]

And he had already prayed to an "inconstant wind," as a "Spirit fierce," "Make me thy lyre. . . . Be through my lips to unawakened earth The trumpet of a prophecy!"[158] Still earlier (Koszul thinks 1817) in an "Essay on Christianity" Shelley had written this remarkably devout passage:

There is a Power by which we are surrounded, like the atmosphere in which some motionless lyre is suspended, which visits with its *breath* our silent chords, at will. Our most *imperial* and *stupendous* qualities—those on which the majesty and the power of humanity is erected . . . are the passive slaves of some higher and more omnipresent Power. This Power is God. And those who have seen God, have, in the period of their purer and more perfect nature, been harmonized by their own will to so exquisite consentaneity of powers as to give forth divinest melody when the breath of universal being sweeps over their frame.[159]

Compare what he says at the end of his "Defence." Persons in whom the poetic power resides

---

155 *Ibid.*, p. 245. Fowler's translation of the last of these clauses reads: "and the poetry of the sane man vanishes into nothingness before that of the inspired madmen." (*Loeb Classical Library*, London, 1933.)

156 Shawcross, *op. cit.*, p. 164. Shelley then goes on to quote the sentence from Tasso used in the "Defence": "No one deserves the name of Creator save God and the Poet."

157 "Defence," pp. 566, 561-562.

158 "Ode to the West Wind," stanza V.

159 Koszul, *op. cit.*, pp. 18-19. Underlined as in MS.

may often, as far as regards many portions of their nature, have little apparent correspondence with that spirit of good of which they are the ministers. But even whilst they deny and abjure, they are compelled to serve, the power which is seated on the throne of their own soul. . . . Poets are the hierophants of an unapprehended inspiration . . . the words which express what they understand not, the trumpets which sing to battle, and feel not what they inspire. . . .[160]

Thus, Socrates in his *Apology* says he found that poets "say many fine things but do not understand the meaning of them," and in the *Ion* he says poets are "as it were, possessed by a spirit not their own."[161] That is Shelley's translation; but in the fragment found with the manuscript of his "Defence," he has brought this statement even closer to his own phrasing by translating it "possessed by a higher power."[162]

S. F. Gingerich (in an essay which in passing criticizes Winstanley's "Platonism in Shelley" for trying to find Platonism where it is doubtful) remarks that to Shelley

the pure, the great, and the mighty poets are the most helpless as individuals. . . . This is the most characteristic contribution of *The Defence of Poetry* to criticism . . . nowhere in modern criticism is there such an insistence on the idea that the poet, when he writes supremely, is the passive instrument of cosmic processes, of the Absolute.[163]

But this should be qualified. It is probably true that if we think only of "modern criticism" and approach Shelley's theory by proceeding through his poetry, such passivity as that expressed in the phrases we have quoted from his "Ode to the West Wind" will seem "characteristic." But if we turn directly from Plato to the "Defence," as Shelley did, we must feel that it is less important as a piece of original thinking than as a great modern expression of age-old Platonism.

There is a difference; but it is not due to Shelley personally. He stands with the ancient and modern Neo-Platonists against Plato, in considering this irrationality entirely admirable, and to the credit of the poet. The ancient Neo-Platonists systematically emphasized the importance of recognizing a divine Good above even the highest Reason (*Nous*). We find this doctrine again in modern Neo-Platonists like Emerson, and the eighteenth-century translator and commentator, Thomas

---

[160] "Defence," p. 568.
[161] Plato, *Apology*, p. 22; *Ion*, p. 533. (*Essays, Letters,* ed. Mrs. Shelley, I, 282.)
[162] Koszul, *op. cit.*, p. 121.
[163] S. F. Gingerich, *Essays in the Romantic Poets* (New York, 1924), p. 225.

Taylor, whose works introduced the young Shelley to "the esoteric doctrines of the poetry and wisdom of antiquity" wherein "Plato, following the doctrines of Timaeus and Pythagoras, taught also a moral and intellectual system of doctrine, comprehending at once the past, the present, and the future condition of man."[164] To Book X of the *Republic*, where poets are condemned in no uncertain terms, Taylor appends a long note from Proclus (of the fifth century A.D.) who interprets Plato into Neo-Platonic orthodoxy by such simple sophistry as this: "He who calls the poetic genus [sic] divine, cannot also ascribe to it an impious and gigantic opinion respecting divine concerns."[165] The central error in this chain of reasoning is the assumption that if an inspiration is divine it is good, as in Christianity. So Shelley can say, as if these prepositional phrases were synonymous: Poetry "acts in a divine and unapprehended manner, beyond and above consciousness."[166] Apparently it does not occur to him that a divine inspiration might be inferior to a rational decision, as Homer and Athenian drama make clear. Greek humanism differed from Oriental and Medieval piety in thinking that a god may send an evil or deceitful, a disorderly or ridiculous, inspiration, which would contradict the good, the true, and the beautiful. Hence Plato is capable of maintaining both that the poet is divinely inspired and that he should be banned from the ideal state as an evil influence. And in Socrates' assertion that poets are divinely inspired and do not understand the fine things they utter, there is an unmistakable note of contempt which Shelley apparently missed; certainly it has disappeared in Shelley's echo of the same view.

Nevertheless, Plato did say, in a passage Shelley translated thus from the *Republic:* "Of all that is good there can be no other cause than God; but some other cause ought to be discovered for evil."[167] And in the *Phaedrus,* just before describing the "third kind of madness" of those "possessed by the Muses" (in the passage much admired by Shelley and praised in a letter to Peacock), Socrates had said such madness is "superior to a sane mind [*sōphrosyne*], for the one is only of human,

---

[164] "Defence," pp. 551-552. The next sentence treats Christianity as part of this tradition: "Jesus Christ divulged the sacred and eternal truths contained in these views to mankind, and Christianity, in its abstract purity, became the exoteric expression of [these] esoteric doctrines."

[165] Taylor, *Works of Plato* (London, 1804), I, 442.

[166] "Defence," p. 538.

[167] Shelley, translating section 379 from Book II of the *Republic.* (*Essays, Letters,* ed. Mrs. Shelley, I, 309.)

but the other of divine origin." And he asserts, "The divine is beauty, wisdom, goodness, and the like."[168]

Even more significant than the Neo-Platonists' treatment of the *Republic* is their handling of the *Ion.* They are blind to its satire on poets. Its charge that poets are irrationally inspired they turn into praise; and they even ascribe this praise to Plato. Taylor's long first note, from Proclus, to Book X of the *Republic,* says that Plato treats "divine poetry" —the first and best of three kinds—in his *Phaedrus* and *Ion,* where "he most clearly evinces that the poetry of Homer is divine, and, to others that are conversant with it, is the cause of enthusiastic energy."[169] This humorless misreading of Plato is not confined to Romantics and the ancients; it is found also in the Renaissance. Sir Philip Sidney, realizing that Plato must be carefully interpreted if used on the side of poetry, says:

Plato therefore, whose authority I had much rather justly construe than unjustly resist, meant not in general of poets . . . but only meant to drive out those wrong opinions of the Deity. . . . And a man need go no further than to Plato himself to know his meaning; who, in his dialogue called Ion, giveth high and rightly divine commendation unto poetry.[170]

Thus Shelley could find in Taylor, Sidney, and Proclus plenty of precedent for his reading of the *Ion.* Indeed the most enthusiastic admirers of Plato have often been Neo-Platonists. It is not always easy to say at what point they begin to do violence to their master's philosophy. We have what might be called a Platonic Neo-Platonism, derived directly from authentic readings in the Socratic dialogues, by the process of placing preponderant emphasis on certain doctrines expressed in the *Symposium,* the *Phaedo,* the *Phaedrus,* the *Ion,* the *Timaeus,* the *Parmenides,* and the *Republic.* Even when the views are those of Plato, there is a tendency to iron out Plato's complexities, ignore the dramatic quality of his dialogue, to take his myths and his humor with solemn dogmatism. Thomas Taylor, for example, declared, "My principal object in this arduous undertaking has been to unfold all the abstruse and sublime dogmas of Plato, as they are found dispersed in his works."[171] And he did not pretend to accomplish this undertaking unassisted, but

---

[168] *Phaedrus,* 244, 246E. Taylor translates the latter: "that which is divine is beautiful, wise, and good." (III, 322.)

[169] Taylor, *Works of Plato,* I, 441.

[170] Sidney, *Apology,* pp. 42-43.

[171] Taylor, *Works of Plato,* I, cix.

for "the only key by which" this valuable "casket . . . can be unlocked" he turned to Plato's "Greek interpreters,"[172] the ancient Neo-Platonists on whom he bases his extensive footnotes. Shelley in his youth met Plato in English translation accompanied by this Neo-Platonic key. The surprising thing is the extent to which his use of Plato is independent of these "esoteric doctrines." We have cited a number of Shelley's views which are Neo-Platonic; but so far we have met very little that is not also to be found somewhere in Plato. Even when the tone and emphasis is changed, or where the full meaning of Plato as revealed elsewhere is left out of account, there is a large area held in common by Plato and the Neo-Platonists. We can hardly deny that these views are Platonic, even though we may prefer the richer Platonism of Socrates.

---

[172] *Ibid.*, I, Dedication to the Duke of Norfolk.

XI. *Poetry not Things Made by Art*

Poems are not for Shelley *objets d'art*. Poetry is not a form. For example, poetry can be *expressed* in drama.[173] Unlike Aristotle and Sidney, Shelley does not consider the poet to be a poet in virtue of what he makes. The word, said Sidney, came from the Greek *poiein*, "which is 'to make'; wherein I know not whether by luck or wisdom we Englishmen have met with the Greeks in calling him a maker," a "high and incomparable title."[174] Shelley, perhaps following Sidney's lead, in his first paragraph mentions the word *poiein*, but defines it as "the principle of synthesis" which "has for its objects those forms which are common to universal nature and existence itself"[175]—shall we say, Platonic ideas? Reading Shelley without any knowledge of Greek, or of Sidney, one might get the impression that *poiein* meant, originally, "imagination." For Shelley, the *work* of art is inferior to art as inspiration. In this he is close to Plotinus, who said, concerning "The Intellectual Beauty," that the form of a statue is in the designer before entering the stone.

The beauty, therefore, exists in a far higher state in the art; that original beauty is not transferred; what comes over is a derivative. . . . Art, then, must itself be beautiful in a far higher and purer degree, since it is the seat and source of that beauty; in the degree in which the beauty is diffused by entering into matter is so much weaker than that concentrated in unity.[176]

Shelley says:

When composition begins, inspiration is already on the decline, and the most glorious poetry that has ever been communicated to the world is probably a feeble shadow of the original conceptions of the poet. . . . This instinct and intuition of the poetical faculty is still more observable in the plastic and pictorial arts . . . and the very mind which directs the

---

173 "Defence," p. 544: "The drama, so long as it continues to express poetry . . ."
174 Sidney, *Apology*, p. 6.
175 "Defence," p. 530.
176 *The Essence of Plotinus*, compiled by Grace Turnbull (New York, 1934), pp. 170-171 (*Ennead*, V, viii).

hands in formation is incapable of accounting to itself for the origin, the gradations, or the media of the process.[177]

If the most glorious poetry is "a feeble shadow," this may be because "the deep truth is imageless."[178] We must not forget that the *Phaedrus* (subtitle: *Concerning the Beautiful*), in spite of all it so beautifully says concerning the art of expression, comes to the conclusion that the written word is ultimately unsatisfactory. Plato's seventh Epistle makes even clearer his dissatisfaction with any attempt to communicate in words the knowledge he considered most valuable:

For it does not at all admit of verbal expression like other studies, but, as a result of continued application to the subject itself and communion therewith, it is brought to birth in the soul on a sudden, as a light that is kindled by a leaping spark, and thereafter it nourishes itself.[179]

"When musing deeply," says Shelley, to Intellectual Beauty, "Sudden, thy shadow fell on me."[180] Shelley, says Gingerich, "arrives, by a sort of instantaneous conversion, suddenly into a full sense of the meaning of Absolute Beauty."[181] With Plato's parallel statements in mind, we may feel that Gingerich goes too far in drawing a complete contrast between the two. Plato, he says, "lays special stress on intellectual discipline, travail, and growth necessary to attain the Beautiful and the Good, which is foreign to Shelley." And he cites the *Republic,* where "the idea of the good appears last of all, and is seen only with an effort."[182] But for Plato we must draw a distinction between the Beautiful and the other transcendental values, as we know from passages in the *Phaedrus* that we have already quoted. Shelley, it is true, does not draw this distinction, but what he says about the Good-True-Beautiful is determined by his conclusions concerning the Beautiful, especially in poetry. And Plato does not claim that poetic beauty is attained only through intellectual discipline and effort.

---

[177] "Defence," pp. 562-563.
[178] *Prometheus Unbound,* II, iv, 116.
[179] Plato, *Epistles,* trans. R. G. Bury, *Loeb Classical Library* (London, 1929), VII, 341D.
[180] "Hymn to Intellectual Beauty," 55, 59.
[181] Gingerich, *op. cit.,* p. 212.
[182] *Ibid.,* p. 205.

XII. *Effluence, Emanation*

Some of Shelley's "Platonism" belongs to the unplatonic aspect of Neo-Platonism. This too we must consider, if we are to indicate accurately the degrees of Shelley's closeness to Plato, and the precise quality of his Platonism. Notopoulos tells us that "Plotinus and the other Neo-Platonists do not appear in Shelley's reading."[183] But he justly says, in another article: "Whereas Platonism places the emphasis on the finite and intelligible, Neo-Platonism places it on the infinite and mystical. Romanticism is attracted to the latter."[184] In that respect, Shelley stands closer to the Neo-Platonists than to Plato, by temperamental affinity. Part of the description of Plotinus by Gilbert and Kuhn reads like a characterization of Shelley:

It sometimes seems as if the flight of Plotinus to the "dear country" "over yonder" was little more than the re-embracing of this country's music and color in a frame of ecstasy. The delicious troubling of which he writes, the savor and fragrance, transparence and splendor, which are to qualify our experience of the "One," Fountain of Form, often seem transported by a change of place rather than of character. . . . In a measure, he retained the flavor and essence of sense while casting out its body.[185]

This is logical enough if Nature is an emanation of the Divine. Even as late as the time of writing his "Defence," Shelley's "Nature" is a concept difficult to distinguish from the Spirit of Beauty, the "One,"—as we can see in his "Adonais." But the Romantic identification of Nature and Spirit, suggesting a Neo-Platonic monism, is less evident in the later than in the earlier writings of Shelley; and least of all in the "Defence."

---

[183] James A. Notopoulos, "The Platonic Sources of Shelley's 'Hymn to Intellectual Beauty',"*PMLA*, LVIII (1943), pp. 582-583.

[184] James A. Notopoulos, "Shelley and Thomas Taylor," *PMLA*, LI (1936), p. 508. This article shows that Shelley used the annotated translation of Plato by the Neo-Platonist Taylor.

[185] Katharine Gilbert and Helmut Kuhn, *A History of Esthetics* (New York, 1939), p. 116.

I am tempted to say that it is a Platonic essay written by a Pantheist; but that would be to stretch Shelley upon a Procrustes bed of systematic terminology that does not fit him.

Different scholars define very differently the boundary between pure Plato and pure Neo-Platonism. But few would deny that one of the characteristics of the latter is the idea of *effluence*. "It looks upon the world as an *overflow*, as a diffusion of the divine life. . . . The universe emanates from the absolute as light emanates from the sun."[186] As Thomas Taylor puts it, "All intellects emanate from one first intellect; all souls from one first soul; all natures blossom from one first nature; and all bodies proceed from the vital and luminous body of the world."[187] On the *Phaedrus* he says, "Socrates speaks concerning all-various beauty . . . he ascends to the intelligible fountain itself of beauty, to the God of love, and to the beautiful itself," and Beauty "is, as it were, a light emitted from the fountain of intelligibles."[188] His "Introduction" to his own translation, *Select Works of Plotinus* (1817), ends with a note concerning Plotinus on Intellectual Beauty, *peri tou noētou kallous*, or as he translates it, "On intelligible beauty." The note says, "The heaven which Plotinus here celebrates as the same with the intelligible world, and the supreme intellect, belongs, accurately speaking, to that divine order which is denominated by the Chaldaean theologists *noētos kai noeros, intelligible and at the same time intellectual*."[189] Elsewhere he quotes Proclus as saying that the best life of the soul connects "its own light with that of the Gods, and that which is most uniform in its own essence and life, with *the one* which is above all essence and life.[190] That which is second" best, on the other hand, "placing intellect and science as the principles of its energy. . . ."[191]

So for Shelley poetry ascends "to bring light and fire from those

---

[186] Alfred Weber and R. B. Perry, *History of Philosophy* (New York, 1925), pp. 128, 131, speaking of the *Enneads* written by Plotinus and published by Porphyry.

[187] Taylor, *Works of Plato*, I, lvii ("General Introduction").

[188] *Ibid.*, III, 286, 327 (the latter a note to "we then saw splendid beauty" [*Phaedrus*, 250]).

[189] Thomas Taylor, *Select Works of Plotinus* (London, 1895), lxxiii.

[190] Compare *Republic*, VI, 509B, "the good may be said to be not only the author of knowledge of all things known, but of their being and essence, and yet the good is not essence, but far exceeds essence in dignity and power." This is compared to the sun as source of visibility as well as of "generation and nourishment."

[191] Taylor, *Works of Plato*, I, 438.

eternal regions where the owl-winged faculty of calculation dare not ever soar."[192] Notice that there is not only en*light*enment, but fire. Each poetic word "is as a spark, a burning atom of inextinguishable thought. . . . A great poem is a fountain forever overflowing with the waters of wisdom and delight;" and no one person or epoch will exhaust "all its divine effluence."[193] And of the poet he writes,

> the pure spirit shall flow
> Back to the burning fountain whence it came,
> A portion of the Eternal, which must glow
> Through time and change, unquenchably the same[194]

Joseph Warren Beach has pointed out that this conception is found in Plotinus, whom he quotes: "As if from universal fire one should be a vast and another a diminutive fire; while in the mean time all the various gradations would proceed from universal fire, or rather from that which is the source of this general fire."[195]

If the individual spirit is an overflow from the divine, one corollary follows which we find in Shelley and prominently in Emerson: that we should love what is within—the Oversoul—in the words of Shelley's "On Love," "a soul within our soul."[196] Plotinus says, "Anyone possessed by God has but to bring that Divine-within before his consciousness and at once he sees an image of himself lifted to a better beauty."[197] Hence Shelley can speak of "that ideal perfection" which "everyone feels to be the internal" (not *eternal*, as we would expect of a Platonist not Neo) "type of all that he loves" and admires. The mind, under the influence of rhythm and wisdom, "pours itself forth . . . into the universal element."[198] We do not need to assume that Shelley had read any of the passages I have quoted from the Neo-Platonists. F. C. Prescott says Shelley

gives us what amounts to a new and independent revelation of religious

---

[192] "Defence," p. 561.

[193] *Ibid.*, p. 556.

[194] "Adonais," 338-341.

[195] Joseph Warren Beach, *The Concept of Nature in Nineteenth-Century English Poetry* (New York, 1936), p. 265.

[196] Shawcross, *op. cit.*, p. 44.

[197] *Essence of Plotinus,* p. 177 (*Ennead,* V, viii).

[198] "Defence," pp. 543, 536. Concerning his Neo-Platonism, M. H. Abrams, in *The Mirror and the Lamp* (Norton Library, N.Y. 1958), p. 129, says Shelley "sometimes turns out to express not only Platonic Ideas, but also human passions, and other mental materials, which he describes in the alien psychology of English empiricism."

truth, embodying this in a series of surprisingly beautiful mythical or fictional creations. Shelley's religion was the product of a fresh imaginative apprehension of man's relation to the world of spirit. . . . The Holy Ghost . . . was to Shelley a vivid present reality.[199]

Professor Barnard quotes this passage, and declares, flatly, "In Shelley's religion, Imagination corresponds to the Christian doctrine of Grace."[200] But we go too far if we assume an identity between Grace and the Power which in Shelley's view takes possession of the poetic soul. We must keep in mind the Platonic psychology, whereby the good in a man is his own real *self*. And even if Plato thought the Muses' frenzy transported a poet out of himself, Neo-Platonists from Plotinus to Emerson have felt that such divine inspiration transports a poet into his still deeper Self. And we must recognize in Shelley, to the end, an element of Nature worship, in contrast to the Christian dogmas concerning Grace as a supplement to, or even a destruction of, Nature in man. What Basil Willey says in *The Seventeenth Century Background* could have a broad application: He points out that the Platonists were opposed to the orthodox depreciation of human nature and human reason in the doctrine of the Fall, and, since spiritual processes are natural, they "could not accept the view expressed in the traditional insistence upon *supernatural* grace, that there was no 'natural light' left to the sons of Adam since the Fall."[201]

Rejecting the idea that Shelley is talking about Christian Grace, must we swing to the other extreme and say that he holds to a Pantheism, even at the end of his life, which is incompatible with his diverse genuine Platonism? I think not. He is too harshly critical of physical and social reality. Whatever he may have been earlier, at this stage of his career his apparent Pantheism springs from his loose formulation of his thought, and from the vague diction so common among the Romantics. For example: For Shelley what *is* the essence of poetry? Beauty? The Universal? "Living Images"? "Inextinguishable Thought"? The difficulty of establishing a precise answer from his text illustrates a vagueness that is itself far from Platonic. This is related to his very unplatonic deficiency in mathematical ability. The friend of his school days, Hogg, writes: "He rejected with marvellous impatience every mathematical discipline that was offered; no problem could awaken the slightest

---

[199] F. C. Prescott, *Poetry and Myth* (New York, 1927), p. 185.
[200] Ellsworth Barnard, *Shelley's Religion* (Minneapolis, 1937), p. 264.
[201] *Op. cit.*, p. 136.

curiosity, nor could he be made sensible of the beauty of any theorem. The method of demonstration had no charms for him. . . ."[202]

He may be contrasted even with Plotinus, who said, for example, "Good men have no other love than for the Absolute and Authentic Good and never follow random loves of a different kind."[203] But theoretically, of course, as he fell in love with one woman after another Shelley was always pursuing successive manifestations of the same divine Beauty. At last, shortly after writing "Epipsychidion," he admitted, "the person whom it celebrates was a cloud instead of a Juno. . . . The error . . . consists in seeking in a mortal image the likeness of what is perhaps eternal."[204] But he acts as if "caprice and appetite" are noble "sentiment and passion" when not "divested of imagination."[205]

In Shelley, as we move away from what is strictly Plato we reach something that is, I am afraid, sometimes called "Platonism," but is not really even unplatonic Neo-Platonism. But we find more of this in his life than in his writing, more in his poetry than in his prose, more in his early career than later. "A Defence of Poetry" is by no means a rebellious break with the Classical tradition.

---

[202] T. J. Hogg, *Life of Percy Bysshe Shelley* (London, 1858), I, 108.
[203] *Essence of Plotinus*, p. 96 (*Ennead*, III, v).
[204] Letter to John Gisborne, June 18, 1822. (*Letters*, ed. Ingpen, II, 976.)
[205] "Defence," p. 545.

XIII. *Shelley's Renaissance Platonism*

It is easy to emphasize the peculiarly Romantic doctrines of Shelley to such an extent that we shut out the great amount of Renaissance Platonism in his "Defence." After all, it is mainly a splendid expression of ideas that were old even at the time of the Revival of Learning. In it he praises Greek culture in a way that would have delighted the Renaissance humanists. Like them he was a translator, an adapter, an omnivorous reader of Classical texts. He wrote a characteristically Renaissance praise of Plato and Epicurus (and criticism of scholastic philosophy) in "On the Revival of Literature"—"Plato the wisest, the profoundest, and Epicurus, the most humane and gentle among the ancients."[206] Of Athens he says in his "Defence," "never was blind strength and stubborn form so disciplined and rendered subject to the will of man, or that will less repugnant to the dictates of the beautiful and the true, as during the century which preceded the death of Socrates."[207] In his manuscript he had said, in addition, "never was such joy of life felt so intensely; never were so many individuals so free to speak or think or feel as the spirit within them dictated."[208] He adopts a Renaissance attitude toward erotic poets—neither a naturalistic glorification nor a Puritan condemnation. This is especially clear in the manuscript statement: "There is nothing in itself vicious or wrong in sensual pleasures, or unworthy in passions. . . ." The same evaluation is present in the "Defence":

It is not what the erotic poets have, but what they have not, in which their imperfection consists. . . . For the end of social corruption is to destroy all sensibility to pleasure. . . . At the approach to such a period, poetry ever addresses itself to those faculties which are the last to be destroyed. . . .

---

[206] Shawcross, *op. cit.*, p. 119.
[207] "Defence," p. 541.
[208] Koszul, *op. cit.*, p. 88.

Poetry ever communicates all the pleasure which men are capable of receiving: it is ever still the light of life. . . .[209]

He justifies earthly love and beauty in terms of heavenly love and beauty, in a thoroughly Renaissance fashion; that is, by using Plato, leaning heavily on the *Phaedrus* and Diotima's advice in the *Symposium* for him "who aspires to love rightly," rising to the Absolute, the "wide ocean of beauty," or as Shelley mistranslates it, adding a word, the "wide ocean of intellectual beauty."[210]

Next to Plato's own writings, the most important source of Platonism for Shelley—and for most readers in English-speaking countries—would certainly be the Renaissance authors: Sir Philip Sidney, Edmund Spenser (especially his *Four Hymns*), John Milton, Francis Bacon, all of whom Shelley read enthusiastically, as he did Boccaccio, Petrarch (especially his *Triumphs*), and other Italians of the Renaissance.[211] Klibansky, tracing the continuity of the Platonic tradition, says that Petrarch's Platonism which began the Florentine movement was based on Latin authors and on the Medieval Latin Plato.

Ficino, the outstanding figure in Renaissance Platonism, far from considering himself as resuscitating a forgotten philosophical creed, is fully conscious of being the descendant of a long line of Latin Platonists. . . . When he calls Augustine "the man of divine genius, who gave the truest expression of the sublimity of Plato," he is at one with Petrarch.[212]

The Greek text which Shelley used in translating Plato's *Symposium* was the Bipont edition *cum Marsilii Ficini Interpretatione*.[213] And Ficino's interpretations Neo-Platonized the master's meaning, as did Thomas Taylor's at the end of the eighteenth century. Indeed, Taylor was merely following Ficino in using Neo-Platonism as a key to "unfold all the abstruse and sublime dogmas of Plato," in spite of the fact that in dedicating his work to the Duke of Norfolk, Taylor wrote that "The patronage likewise of the Medici was more confined than that of your

---

[209] "Defence," p. 547.

[210] Section 210.

[211] Paul Shorey, in *Platonism Ancient and Modern* (Berkeley, 1938), pp. 182, 234, says, "the Baconian forms turn out . . . to be the Platonic ideas," and deplores Macaulay's "sophistical contrast between the Platonic and the Baconian method."

[212] R. Klibansky, *The Continuity of the Platonic Tradition During the Middle Ages* (London, 1939), pp. 31-32, 42.

[213] James A. Notopoulos, "Note on the Text of Shelley's Translation of the 'Symposium'," *Modern Language Review*, XXXIV (1939), p. 421.

Grace: for by giving Plato to the public in a Roman garb, unattended with his Greek interpreters in the same garb" they gave "an invaluable casket, but without the only key by which it can be unlocked."[214] Of course, as a matter of fact the Renaissance did receive its Plato along with a strong dose of Neo-Platonism. The Elizabethans were tinged with it. That is why we do not need to assume that Shelley read Plotinus or Proclus at all, in order to account for those relatively few passages where he must be called only Neo-Platonic, not Platonic. But for the most part, Shelley would find his genuine Plato (read of course in the Greek original) supported, illuminated, beautified, raised to the seventh heaven, by the contagious enthusiasm of great English verse, and by the glowing prose of Renaissance humanists. In Shelley's "Defence" there is hardly anything that can be set off as peculiarly "Romantic Platonism." (This I confess was something of a surprise to me; for I once expected to be able to find here something as different from sixteenth-century Platonism as Modernism is different from sixteenth-century Puritanism.) Almost everything called "Romantic" in his Platonism can be matched in Plotinus, or in older English poetry, such as the following from the beginning of Spenser's "Hymne of Heavenly Beautie":

> Vouchsafe then, O thou most almightie Spright,
> From whom all gifts of wit and knowledge flow,
> To shed into my breast some sparkling light
> Of thine eternall Truth, that I may show
> Some little beames to mortall eyes below,
> Of that immortall beautie . . .
> That with the glorie of so goodly sight,
> The hearts of men, which fondly here admyre
> Faire seeming shewes, and feed on vaine delight,
> Transported with celestiall desyre
> Of those faire formes, may lift themselves up hyer,
> And learne to love with zealous humble dewty
> Th'eternall fountaine of that heavenly beauty.

This poetry, written two centuries before Shelley was born, integral part of a poem so heavily and literally indebted to the *Phaedrus* and the *Symposium,* shows how erroneous it would be to ascribe to the Romantic Movement the distinction between Plato and Shelley drawn by Barnard:

Shelley does not share Plato's rationalistic bent. Plato regards the highest good as Idea, Shelley as Spirit. . . . It is not Intellectual Beauty but Spiritual

---

[214] Taylor, *Works of Plato,* I, Dedication.

Beauty to which Shelley's *Hymn* is dedicated, as are "Life of Life" and *Epipsychidion;* . . . the end sought is not the contemplation of the Idea of Beauty, but the complete union with the living Spirit of Beauty.[215]

This is the kind of thing I mean in speaking of Shelley's Renaissance Platonism.

But Shelley would not agree with Renaissance literary theory in claiming that the poet is pre-eminent in teaching "moral doctrine," as Sidney does.[216] Equally enthusiastic over the poet's function of "delightful teaching,"[217] he did not think that the best method was forthright didacticism. "A poet," he says, "would do ill to embody his own conceptions of right and wrong, which are usually those of his place and time, in his poetical creations."[218] Thus, in general, Shelley rejects the neoclassicism while following the Platonism of the Renaissance.

He did not reject what the Renaissance took over from the high Middle Ages, when "Love became a religion, the idols of whose worship were ever present." The verses of the Provençal Trouveurs "are as spells, which unseal the inmost enchanted fountains of delight" and "Dante understood the secret things of love even more than Petrarch." Like the Renaissance poets and those who created Courtly Love, he notes "how the gentleness and the elevation of mind connected with these sacred emotions can render men more amiable, more generous and wise."[219] But, "it were superfluous to explain how." So it is, after Plato. For while the Medieval cult feminized the worship, the basic argument for the beneficent effect of love on character is found in Plato. For example, in the *Symposium*, Phaedrus speaking, Shelley translating:

For neither birth, nor wealth, nor honours, can awaken in the minds of men the principles which should guide those who from their youth aspire to an honourable and excellent life, as Love awakens them. . . . There is none so worthless whom Love cannot impel, as it were, by a divine inspiration, towards virtue . . . as Homer says: The God breathes vigour into certain heroes—so Love breathes into those who love, the spirit which is produced from himself.[220]

Love, says Shelley, "found a worthy poet in Plato alone of all the ancients," and "the dominion of love" is the "sublimest victory over sen-

---

[215] Barnard, *Shelley's Religion*, pp. 287-288.
[216] Sidney, *Apology*, p. 31.
[217] *Ibid.*, p. 11; cf. Shelley ("Defence," p. 538): from poetry we "receive the wisdom which is mingled with its delight."
[218] "Defence," p. 540.
[219] *Ibid.*, pp. 552-553.
[220] Sections 178-179 (*Essays, Letters,* ed. Mrs. Shelley, I, 85, 86, 87).

suality and force."[221] Thus the religion of love, which seems so romantic, can be traced clear back through the Christian Platonists to Socrates— or to Diotima herself. In *Platonism Ancient and Modern,* Professor Shorey says:

This doctrine of Platonic love included in its higher and lower manifestations the *henosis* of Plotinus, the religious raptures of St. Francis, Dante's love for Beatrice, Petrarch's love for Laura, the poet's eye in fine frenzy rolling, Spinoza's intellectual love of God, and everything that the eighteenth century . . . stigmatized as enthusiasm.[222]

The tradition of Platonism as a whole finds expression in Shelley's essay: chiefly Plato, of course, but with contributions from ancient Neo-Platonists, with both these ancient sources poetically restated in Renaissance Italy and England, to be revived by later enthusiasts like Thomas Taylor. But the "Defence" looks forward as well as backward. Its theory is "perennial."

---

[221] "Defence," p. 553.
[222] *Op. cit.,* p. 134.

XIV. *Democratic Platonism*

Corruption must utterly have destroyed the fabric of human society before poetry can ever cease. The sacred links of that chain have never been entirely disjoined, which descending through the minds of many men is attached to those great minds, whence as from a magnet the invisible effluence is sent forth, which at once connects, animates, and sustains the life of all. It is the faculty which contains within itself the seeds at once of its own and of social renovation.[223]

A *propos* of this statement in Shelley's "Defence," we find in the manuscript a note, "This is the language of Plato." And with the manuscript was found a compressed paraphrase of the relevant passage from Plato's *Ion*:

For a divine power moves you, as that of the magnet; which not only can draw iron rings to itself but can endow them with a similar power of attraction to draw other rings, until a long chain of rings is attached to each other; and all is attached to the stone itself.—Thus poetry, being itself divinely inspired, communicates this inspiration to others, until a long chain is made, every link of which is a human spirit.[224]

Turning to the published translation by Shelley of the whole *Ion* we find almost all of this, in slightly different words, except the last, which takes the place of "so the Muse, communicating through those whom she has first inspired, to all others capable of sharing in the inspiration, the influence of that first enthusiasm, creates a chain and a succession."[225] It is to be noted, however, that in the "Defence" only the figure of speech, not the meaning, is Plato's. The sacred chain sketched by Socrates indicates the dependence of audience on rhapsodist, rhapsodist on the poet, poet on divine inspiration. Doubtless Shelley agreed absolutely with this, but his actual use of "the language of Plato" here is rather

---

[223] "Defence," p. 548; see Koszul, *op. cit.*, p. 88.
[224] *Ibid.*, p. 121.
[225] Shelley's translation of Plato's *Ion*, sec. 533 (*Essays, Letters*, ed. Mrs. Shelley, I, 282).

to show that poetry's "invisible effluence" contains the seeds of "social renovation," a task which would not by Plato be assigned to poetry. There is nothing about the fabric of society in the *Ion* passage. Shelley's use of Plato for Godwinian ends in this way represents a significant development. With the great Victorians in mind we may add that the use of Plato as a basis for advocating social change is the most important nineteenth-century modification of the Platonic tradition in England.

But during the nineteenth century both conservatives and utilitarians used Plato; Shelley was neither.

In constructing his "Defence of Poetry" Shelley answers the four points his letter to Ollier distinguished in Peacock's essay, and then turns to the *Ion* for positive doctrine in favor of the poets, with a paragraph beginning "Poetry is indeed something divine," a restatement of the *Ion*, "poems are not human . . . but divine."[226] But just before this transition he has been answering the utilitarian objection to poetry on the utilitarians' own ground: "The production and assurance of pleasure in this highest sense is true utility. Those who produce and preserve this pleasure are poets or poetical philosophers."[227] This portion of his argument rises to the conclusion that

The functions of the poetical faculty are two-fold; by one it creates new materials of knowledge and power and pleasure; by the other it engenders in the mind a desire to reproduce and arrange them according to a certain rhythm and order which may be called the beautiful and the good.

As to the first of these two functions, the manuscript makes the issue clearer. He had referred to Peacock's "array of all the denominations of the subordinate arts of life which are employed upon working out of the elements originally furnished by the poetical faculty, materials of knowledge and power. And he [Peacock] protests against an attempt to create new elements by that only process. . . ."[228] By leaving this out of the final version he has cut down his treatment of this function of creation that *precedes* the work of utilitarian sciences, thus throwing more emphasis on the other function which comes after the sciences have done their work. But this leaves two sentences (crucial in his answer to the utilitarian objection) without the support of the passage I have just quoted from the manuscript, and consequently easy to mis-

---

[226] "Defence," p. 561; *Ion,* 534 (*Essays, Letters,* ed. Mrs. Shelley, I, 284).
[227] "Defence," p. 559.
[228] Koszul, *op. cit.,* pp. 105-106.

interpret: "The poetry of these systems of [scientific and political] thought, is concealed by the accumulation of facts and calculating processes." (Poetry here means approximately imagination.) "There is no want of knowledge respecting what is wisest and best in morals, government, and political economy, or at least, what is wiser and better than what men now practise and endure."[229] This knowledge is *not* supplied by the material and positive sciences, as might seem at first reading, but by creative imagination, nourished on the Biblical and Classical literary traditions.[230] It is easy to misread these two sentences and think that they are saying we need the poetic feeling to put into practice the knowledge supplied by science, for immediately without any transition Shelley is talking about the other, the second, of the "functions of the poetical faculty," by quoting "I dare not . . ." from Macbeth and adding, "We want the creative faculty to imagine that which we know; we want the generous impulse to act that which we imagine; we want the poetry of life. . . ."[231] Imaginative insight is needed first to supply "the elements" of wisdom, and then after "the subordinate arts" have been "employed upon working" them out, imagination is again required for "just distribution"—"The cultivation of poetry is never more to be desired than at periods when, from an excess of the selfish and calculating principle, the accumulation of the materials of external life exceed the quantity of the power of assimilating them. . . ."[232] Shelley's dissatisfaction with the orthodox economics of the early nineteenth century does not look at all impractical today. But he does not keep his social thinking on the economic level; society should be dominated by love, not money. In his manuscript we find written, and cancelled, "Poetry is the representation of the benevolent principle in man,"[233] and this should be kept in mind when he asks why the Industrial Revolution had not advanced democracy:

To what but a cultivation of the mechanical arts in a degree disproportioned to the presence of the creative faculty is to be attributed the abuse of all invention for abridging and combining labour, to the exasperation of the inequality of mankind? From what other cause has it arisen that the dis-

---

[229] "Defence," p. 560.
[230] *Ibid.*, p. 559: "it exceeds all imagination to conceive what would have been the moral condition of the world . . . if Hebrew poetry had never been translated; if a revival of the study of Greek literature had never taken place . . . if the poetry of the religion of the ancient world had been extinguished."
[231] *Ibid.*, p. 560.
[232] *Ibid.*, p. 561.
[233] Koszul, *op. cit.*, p. 106.

coveries which should have lightened, have added a weight to the curse imposed on Adam? Poetry, and the principle of Self, of which money is the visible incarnation, are the God and the Mammon of the world.[234]

The topic sentence of the same paragraph has often been read as if it were two ways of saying the same thing (after the manner of Hebrew poetry); but the manuscript omissions we have quoted show that he is thinking of two ways in which the creative imagination has a practical and utilitarian value, both in supplying "those first principles which belong to the imagination"[235] and in applying the benefits of science "to the actual lives of living men."[236] This topic sentence reads: "We have more moral, political and historical wisdom, than we know how to reduce into practice; we have more scientific and economical knowledge than can be accommodated to the just distribution of the produce which it multiplies." In short, "the root and blossom of all other systems of thought" is what Shelley means by "poetry," that is, creative imagination.[237]

"The rich have become richer, and the poor have become poorer; and the vessel of the state is driven between the Scylla and Charybdis of anarchy and despotism."[238] Socrates also deplores the society which honors wealth: "such a State is not one, but two States, the one of poor, the other of rich men; and they are living on the same spot and always conspiring against one another."[239] But the *Republic* makes it clear that Plato was no democrat. Shelley assimilated Plato to his own mind more than he had any right to, when he wrote: "The principle of equality had been discovered and applied by Plato in his *Republic*, as the theoretical rule of the mode in which the materials of pleasure and of power, produced by the common skill and labour of human beings, ought to be distributed among them."[240] To back up Shelley's ascription of egalitarianism to Plato, Cook's edition quotes a long passage from the

---

[234] "Defence," p. 560.
[235] *Ibid.*, p. 558.
[236] I have quoted this not from Shelley but from Wild's *Plato's Theory of Man* (p. 29), contrasting the theoretical truths of Aristotle with the literary works of Plato, by which "our wills are stirred to that aspiration without which such knowledge would never be achieved in the first place, nor ever applied to the actual lives of living men." He stresses the practical emphasis in Plato's thought. The double parallel with Shelley's exposition is remarkable.
[237] "Defence," p. 560.
[238] *Ibid.*, p. 558.
[239] *Republic*, VIII, 551.
[240] "Defence," p. 551.

Republic that refers only to the auxiliaries, which Cook makes to sound as if it applied to all the citizens. He accomplishes this by omitting, in the middle, one sentence beginning, "And they alone of all the citizens may not touch or handle silver or gold. . . ."[241] The whole passage is preceded by the argument that God has framed the citizens differently. "Some of you have the power of command" and "our auxiliaries, being stronger than our citizens," might "become savage tyrants" unless they had "a really good education."[242] His ideal is a sharply graded class system—open to talent. Shelley is certainly misreading Plato's text. But can we say that democracy, like poetic idealism, is a legitimate derivative of Platonism? At first we would answer easily, no. But considering how many political liberals and revolutionaries, from the seventeenth century on, have read, and used, Plato, or philosophers who "Platonized," we meet a paradox that may give us pause.

Whatever the logic of it may be, Shelley was a social revolutionary before he was a Platonist. The immediate source of his equalitarian democracy was of course the French Revolution and its principles, especially as they are expressed by Godwin. But his critical principles he did not derive from Godwin or the French rationalists. Indeed, he was turning sharply away from the French by the time he wrote his "Defence of Poetry," where he says: "But whilst the sceptic destroys gross superstitions, let him spare to deface, as some of the French writers have defaced, the eternal truths charactered upon the imaginations of men."[243] (This is a Platonism thoroughly compatible with the "Declaration of Independence.") And he wrote, April 11, 1822, "the doctrines of the French, and Material Philosophy, are as false as they are pernicious."[244] What Shelley did was to effect a union of idealistic philosophy with liberalism and democracy, characteristic of English and American political development, in contrast to the materialism of the equalitarian movement on the Continent—even to this day.

Shelley's political position is closer to that of such representative American thinkers as Jefferson and Emerson, than to that of modern British democratic idealists. For the British ultimately fused the legacy

---

[241] *Shelley's Defence of Poetry,* ed. Albert S. Cook (Boston, 1891), pp. 72-73, the omitted sentence I have quoted being in the same translation used in Cook's notes, *Republic,* III, 417.

[242] *Republic,* III, 415-416.

[243] "Defence," p. 558.

[244] *Letters,* II, 959-960.

of the French Revolution with the principles of its greatest critic, Edmund Burke. Hence the traditionalism and gradualness of British socialism, or the radicalism of their Tory opponents, would seem as strange to Shelley as to the typical American.

All this is part of the "Defence of Poetry." To ignore it is to drop the political dimension out of that critical philosophy, and pare Shelley down in the direction of aestheticism. It must be remembered that Shelley has had an ardent following for his left-wing political position from his earliest successful publication, *Queen Mab*, down to the generation of Upton Sinclair, who says, "with him perished the finest mind the English race had produced."[245] An article called "A Defense of Poetry," by Horace Gregory, in the *New Republic*, says,

the synthesis that Shelley defined as poetry is an eternal celebration of the human spirit as opposed to the celebration of ritual, the obscene act of worship before an empty altar. . . . It was necessary to him as a poet (a poet in the sense that he conceived Lucretius and Milton to be) to accept his share of human responsibility—the very responsibility that the critics of our day are trying to divorce from the function of poetry.[246]

Gregory's article was written in answer to one by Allen Tate which argued that poetry should be "pure" from politics, and that "art arises in particulars," thus locating the object of poetic interest in what his fellow critic, John Crowe Ransom, calls the World's Body. Thus in the twentieth century, the anti-Platonists in American literary criticism clash with the Shelleyans.

What is the function of poetry in an age that has witnessed such triumphs of science and "the mechanic arts"? Similar, in Shelley's view, to that which it served when Classical civilization broke down, "And the world would have fallen into utter anarchy and darkness, but that there were found poets among the authors of the Christian and chivalric systems of manners and religion, who created forms of opinion and action never before conceived."[247] And so again. For at the end of his essay Shelley announces, "The second part"—which he never wrote—would include "a defence of the attempt [by poets of the new epoch] to idealize," i.e. to render more ideal,

---

[245] *Mammonart* (Pasadena, 1925), p. 183.

[246] Horace Gregory, "A Defence of Poetry," *New Republic*, LXXVI (Oct. 11, 1933), pp. 235, 238. Cf. Allen Tate, "Poetry and Politics," *New Republic*, LXXV (Aug. 2, 1933), p. 310.

[247] "Defence," p. 549.

the modern forms of manners and opinions, and compel them into a sub-ordination to the imaginative and creative faculty. . . . Our own will be a memorable age in intellectual achievements, and we live among such philosophers and poets as surpass beyond comparison any who have appeared since the last national struggle for civil and religious liberty.[248]

Shocked that in a scientific and industrial age, "man, having enslaved the elements, remains himself a slave,"[249] Shelley would have men achieve democratic equality and a richer "internal" culture by a modern application of the ideas of Diotima, recommended in the *Symposium:*

all that intercourse and converse which is conceded by the Gods to men . . . subsists through the intervention of Love; and he who is wise in the science of this intercourse is supremely happy . . . while he is who is wise in any other science or art, remains a mere ordinary slave. . . .

Love is indeed universally all that earnest desire for the possession of happiness and that which is good; the greatest and subtlest love, and which inhabits the heart of every living being. . . .

They whose souls are far more pregnant than their bodes, conceive and produce that which is more suitable to the soul. What is suitable to the soul? Intelligence, and every other power and excellence of the mind; of which all poets, and all other artists who are creative and inventive, are the authors. The greatest and most admirable wisdom is that which regulates the government of families and states, and which is called moderation and justice. Whosoever, therefore, from his youth feels his soul pregnant with the conception of these excellencies, is divine. . . .

And every one who considers what posterity Homer and Hesiod, and the other great poets, have left behind them, the sources of their own immortal memory and renown . . . or what an illustrious progeny of laws Solon has produced . . . would choose rather to be parent of such children than those in a human shape.[250]

Then follows Diotima's advice concerning the "correct system of Love," whereby "such as discipline themselves upon this system" ascend "as on steps" from the love of beautiful forms to beautiful souls and the loveliness of wisdom, through science to beautiful laws and institutions, "until, from the meditation of many [philosophic] doctrines, they arrive at . . . the supreme beauty itself."

"Such a life as this, my dear Socrates," exclaimed the stranger Prophetess, "spent in the contemplation of the beautiful, is the life for men to live . . . to him [who dwells with it] is accorded the prerogative of bringing forth,

---

[248] *Ibid.,* p. 568.
[249] *Ibid.,* p. 560.
[250] *Essays, Letters,* ed. Mrs. Shelley, I, 129, 130, 134, 141, 142 (Shelley's translation, sections 203-209).

not images and shadows of virtue, for he is in contact not with a shadow, but with reality; with virtue itself, in the production and nourishment of which he becomes dear to the Gods. . . ."

Such, O Phaedrus, and my other friends, was what Diotima said. And being persuaded by her words, I have since occupied myself in attempting to persuade others. . . . Wherefore I exhort every one to honour Love.[251]

Diotima's doctrine that Love communicates immortality, Shelley was developing in "Adonais." In the "Defence" he is rather concerned with love "as the root-impulse of all artistic, and also of all moral or social activity"[252]—thus Shawcross states a view that he notes in the *Symposium,* and in Shelley.

This most unquestionable Platonism, direct from Plato, is also Shelley's most modern and democratic contribution to the tradition. He develops it as follows:

The great secret of morals is love; or a going out of our own nature, and an identification of ourselves with the beautiful which exists in thought, action, or person, not our own. A man, to be greatly good, must imagine intensely and comprehensively; he must put himself in the place of another and of many others; the pains and pleasures of his species must become his own. The great instrument of moral good is the imagination. . . . Poetry enlarges the circumference of the imagination by replenishing it with thoughts of ever new delight. . . .[253]

Shelley's defence of the social usefulness of imaginative literature is great not for its orginality, but as an echo—and a light unto eternity!

---

[251] *Ibid.,* I, 146, 147 (sections 211-212).
[252] Shawcross, *op. cit.,* xxix.
[253] "Defence," p. 540.